Experience
Skype to the Max

The Essential Guide to the World's Leading
Internet Communications Platform

Jim Courtney

Experience Skype to the Max: The Essential Guide to the World's Leading Internet Communications Platform

ISBN-13 (pbk): 978-1-4842-0657-7

ISBN-13 (electronic): 978-1-4842-0656-0

Managing Director: Welmoed Spahr
Lead Editor: Gwenan Spearing
Technical Reviewer: Greg Kettell
Editorial Board: Steve Anglin, Mark Beckner, Ewan Buckingham, Gary Cornell,
     Louise Corrigan, Jim DeWolf, Jonathan Gennick, Robert Hutchinson, Michelle Lowman,
     James Markham, Susan McDermott, Matthew Moodie, Jeffrey Pepper, Douglas Pundick,
     Ben Renow-Clarke, Dominic Shakeshaft, Gwenan Spearing, Matt Wade, Steve Weiss
Coordinating Editor: Christine Ricketts
Copy Editor: Linda Seifert
Compositor: SPi Global
Indexer: SPi Global
Artist: SPi Global

Distributed to the book trade worldwide by Springer Science+Business Media New York, 233 Spring Street, 6th Floor, New York, NY 10013. Phone 1-800-SPRINGER, fax (201) 348-4505, e-mail orders-ny@springer-sbm.com, or visit www.springeronline.com. Apress Media, LLC is a California LLC and the sole member (owner) is Springer Science + Business Media Finance Inc (SSBM Finance Inc). SSBM Finance Inc is a **Delaware** corporation.

For information on translations, please e-mail rights@apress.com, or visit www.apress.com.

Apress and friends of ED books may be purchased in bulk for academic, corporate, or promotional use. eBook versions and licenses are also available for most titles. For more information, reference our Special Bulk Sales–eBook Licensing web page at www.apress.com/bulk-sales.

Any source code or other supplementary material referenced by the author in this text is available to readers at www.apress.com. For detailed information about how to locate your book's source code, go to www.apress.com/source-code/.

To my understanding wife, Evelyn, whose patience I often challenged with my passion for everything digital

Disclaimer

The contents of this book reflect the experience the author has gained using IP-based communications applications since 1995, including eight years' experience working with various players in the Skype™ ecosystem—Skype employees, Skype hardware and software partners, participants at various events where Skype is either a sponsor or participant, and bloggers who write about Skype and other IP-based communications.

This book and its contents have not been endorsed or reviewed by Skype. Any views or opinions expressed are entirely views of the author or the cited source only. There has been no endorsement or other form of support for the publication of this book supplied by Microsoft, Skype, and its affiliates other than through content that may arise from activities related to Skype's public relations programs.

This book is based, in part, on communications software licensed, and information published, by Skype at the time of writing. At its sole discretion Skype may add, modify, or remove features and change pricing without notice. Please consult the Skype website for the current features, offerings, and pricing policies. While the author has diligently attempted to provide accurate information, the author takes no responsibility for any errors or omissions, and makes no warranties with respect to the accuracy and completeness of the contents of this book.

The Skype name, associated trademarks and logos and the "S" logo are trademarks of the Microsoft group of companies. The author and Denali InterConneXions NA Inc. is not affiliated, sponsored, authorized, or otherwise associated with or by the Skype group of companies. All other trademarks are the property of their registered owners.

Contents at a Glance

Contents

About the Author

Jim Courtney has over 30 years of sales, marketing, business development management, and consulting experience in the high-technology market space. From operating an IBM 7090/94 at a university computer center to using his iPhone 5 and BlackBerry z30 today, Jim brings a unique perspective on the evolution of various technologies, including the evolution of real-time communications over the Internet since 1995. Formerly associate editor of Skype Journal, he has been editor and publisher of Voice On The Web since early 2009, covering IP-based communications, including Skype as well as the transition to a mobile world through smartphones and tablets.

About the Technical Reviewer

Greg Kettell is a software developer and writer with over 25 years' experience in programming everything from enterprise applications, to websites and single- and multi-player games. He has contributed to numerous books on Windows, Mac, and iOS applications. Greg is an avid photographer and amateur astronomer, and has recently been getting used to the empty nest life in upstate New York with his wife, their dog, and two rambunctious cats.

Acknowledgments

In July 2012 I published the first edition of *Experience Skype to the Max*. Of course because Skype is continuously under development, modifying features, and adding new ones, the book needed an update three years later. In the spring of 2014 I was approached by Apress about the opportunity of authoring such an update, this time with the resources and support of a proven publisher.

I want to thank Gwenan Spearing, Acquisitions Editor at Apress, who approached me initially and championed this edition at Apress; she has also served as the Lead Editor during the authoring and editing process. Gwenan has provided both the support and guidance needed to make this happen. I also would like to acknowledge the participation of Christine Ricketts, Coordinating Editor, who managed all the behind the scenes logistics required to pull the entire team together to produce the final outcome. Finally I need to acknowledge the contributions of the other members of the Apress team, mentioned in the introduction, who ensured both the integrity and readability of the content through their review, copy editing, and proof reading activities. They have all been a pleasure to work with, even when it only involves communicating via Word's Markups and Comments features. On the other hand, Skype Group Chat with Gwenan and Christine proved invaluable in making the communications flow during this process.

I also need to acknowledge the support and patience of my wife, Evelyn, for giving me the leeway to follow the evolution of the Internet as a communications and information delivery tool.

Introduction

As a child growing up we lived in Saskatoon, Saskatchewan, thousands of miles away from our family in Toronto, Ontario. On my father's $2,000/year salary we rarely made calls back to Toronto. Probably on Christmas Day and only for five minutes at $2 or $3 per minute; each spoken word was valuable but costly. Operators had to place the call. Our phone number had at most five digits. Toward the end of our time there the phone companies built a microwave tower network across the country with towers every 50 to 75 miles. The microwave tower network also brought live broadcasting across the country; we could actually watch the last two periods of NHL games on Saturday night from thousands of miles away.

Fast forward eight years later and we moved to London, Ontario where I attended high school. Phone numbers would have two letters and four digits such as GL-2522. And to make saying them easier they would actually be the starting letters of a longer name such as GLadstone. Within five years came the addition of area codes—we lived in 519—and the introduction of Direct Distance Dialing, eliminating the need for an operator. Calls were still expensive at $1 to $5 per minute, depending on distance. Rotary dials were still the standard phone hardware, but they transitioned the phone numbers to seven digits—all numbers—such as 451-2522.

When I moved to the University of Toronto for my Engineering Science studies our residence had one rotary dial phone to be shared amongst all the members of our residence. Gosh, some of the guys would talk to their girlfriends for hours; it was a tension creator. In 1965 (black and white) satellite television allowed us to watch live telecasts from Europe in 40 minute segments as geostationary orbits were not used yet. So we would get segments of Winston Churchill's funeral interrupted by documentaries about his life—and still in black and white only. Overseas long distance calls were prohibitively expensive.

Moving on to Graduate School, where I obtained Master and Ph.D. degrees in Physics, we saw the advent of color television in Canada. And some graduate students would have their own phones in their residence rooms, at some exorbitant cost. The university had installed a central switch. Labs and offices were assigned four digit "extension" numbers that could be dialed for internal calls and you had to dial 9 to start an outbound call. We still had a rotary phone in our apartment and one tended to minimize long distance calling as it was still relatively expensive. My Ph.D. supervisor let us know whenever he saw a long-distance charge against his research grant.

During my time at the University of Toronto I had my first digital computer experience. One night a week I ran the University's IBM 7090 and later 7094 mainframes with nine tape drives and a huge keyboard. I spent a summer at Imperial Oil running linear programming software that determined the fracking output requirements of refineries. You booted the machine using a 36-key switchboard and entered each of about 30 instructions manually (and hoped you didn't make a mistake). Punch cards were read onto tapes via a punch card to tape reader; output was printed on separate chain link printers, which were both huge and clunky and located in a separate room. Calculations related to my thesis were performed on a HP desktop calculator that took up a one foot square footprint.

Having completed graduate school we moved to West Germany where I worked for a scientific instrumentation company. All communications with North America were made using a Telex service; punch out a paper tape and then run it through the machine to send the message that was typed out at the other end. During our 18 months there we made one call back to Canada, using my employer's phone, to tell our parents about the birth of our son. Because it took 18 months to get phone service installed, we never had one. We had to go to a phone booth down the street, put in some coins, and then be abruptly cut off when the coins ran out. And you paid for both local and long distance calls by the minute. Deutsche Telecom was placing the seeds for the rapid adoption of Skype 30 years later.

On moving back to Canada and settling into a townhouse we had to be amongst the first to install a touch-tone phone, for which we paid an extra couple of dollars per month for the privilege of not blistering your finger using a rotary dial. For business it was good etiquette to have a long-distance calling card and not use your customer's phones. Well, with one exception— when I visited a lab in Ottawa my customer would let me use his phone to make calls across the country at no expense over government trunk lines. Most of my calls were to federal research grant recipients, so at least they were to recipients of government money. But it gave me my first taste of the "free" long-distance calling experience.

Over the next 20 years I traveled not only across Canada and the U.S. selling computerized instrumentation and computer peripherals, but also to Hong Kong and Australia where I started to get a feel for the overseas calling experience, including figuring out country codes and time zone differences. While in Sydney we found that the country manager needed to be replaced; that involved several "discrete" calls back to my manager in California. Hotels would have significant charges for making long-distance calls; in fact, they counted on long-distance calling for a significant portion of their revenues to pay for maintaining the hotel switch and then some. When I completed my Executive MBA in 1985 my new employer set me up with one of the first cell phones. It was—a large brick-size device that I could only use in my car and involved significant wiring within the car as there was also a power supply installed in the trunk. You would not make calls when driving because it was too distracting an experience.

During this time I was involved in selling equipment that either used embedded mini-computers or embedded processors. One of the items, a real-time audio spectrum analyzer gave me lots of experience with audio spectrum—that made it easy to understand why telephone calls had such bad audio. I sold the last core memory computer sold in Canada for which a 4KB memory module cost $2,500. And a 15-inch disc platter would hold 4MB of data; the disc drive would be a $5,000 expense. Toward the end of my time in the scientific instrumentation business I bought an Apple][in order to use spreadsheets for budgeting. While completing my MBA I also bought my first Personal Computer—an IBM PC-AT with a 20MB hard disk (about a 6″ cube) and 1MB of RAM; one of my employers actually sold memory expansion cards. That also was my first exposure to multi-tasking, selling a multi-tasking environment for DOS-PCs, which had 386 or later processors that ran each application on internal "virtual machines."

From 1990 to 1994 I ran the Canadian operation of Quarterdeck Office Systems who published the top selling utility for DOS-PCs as well as the DESQview multi-tasking environment. I spent the next two years at their Santa Monica headquarters where we attempted to enter into the Internet software publishing game, including the development of a web browser, having bought a license from the University of Illinois. Windows 95 killed off our business for those two utilities; some other utilities persisted for a couple of years. However the web browser experience taught me a lot about the Internet and its potential. In fact, Quarterdeck even brought out one of the first Internet calling applications, using Voice over Internet Protocol (VoIP) technology (more on that in Chapter 13). However, the Internet infrastructure and PC processor technology were not quite ready for mass adoption. As for the browser, Microsoft introduced Internet Explorer as one component of the Windows 95 operating system, saying the browser was a feature, not an independent application. End of our browser business, even though it contained features, such as tabs, that did not appear in IE or Firefox for another seven or eight years.

On returning to Canada while remnants of Quarterdeck were being sold to Symantec I went into the business plan consulting business, having been exposed to the start-up environment while in California. I would bill customers anywhere from $100 to $500 per month for long-distance calls involved in their activities. And a conference call with five people could run up a $100 to $300 bill in minutes (or maybe an hour or so).

Personal computers continued to advance in processing power; the Internet was evolving from dialup connections to broadband (cable and DSL) services. You could stay constantly connected to the Internet without tying up a phone line. And the first Instant Messaging applications appeared; it frustrated my wife to no end that I was exchanging information with my daughter at a university residence using ICQ and she was not privy to the conversation. But it was my first exposure to the value of ongoing, real-time chat conversations.

I had tended to follow developments in VoIP-based calling; in fact, one of my clients included it with a screen sharing program they offered. But within a year after the launch of Skype in summer 2003 I found myself increasingly using Skype from both my home office and during travels. When I once had to call a client visiting Norway from a customer's office in Santa Barbara, CA without needing to involve the customer's staff and phone system, a key value of Skype hit me. No cost, no worrying about running up a bill, no disruption of the customer's office activities or having to use a calling card, and quite clear voice quality—just needed an Ethernet connection to my laptop. In fact, the staff did not even know I had made an overseas call from their office.

In 2006 I started publishing posts on Skype Journal; we followed the evolution of improved audio quality as well as video calling from a postage stamp size 320 × 240 image to high quality 640 × 480 video at 30 frames per second. We witnessed the expansion of Skype's platform support to Mac PCs and later to mobile smartphones, initially on the early iPhones. And new features evolved; they are discussed in this book.

During this time I also was involved in consulting engagements that involved not only, say, call centers, but also Skype audio and video hardware peripherals and its evolution. I also did testing of HD video cameras using Skype before they were launched and was involved in the testing of Skype for BlackBerry 10. (Yes, I am still a BlackBerry fan but have had lots of exposure to not only their devices, past and present, but also iOS and Android smartphones and tablets.)

So we come to today where we have hand-held smartphones that have significantly more power than those early IBM mainframes - and we can carry them in our pockets without the need for air conditioning (but probably longer battery life). If connected to a car audio, it used a hands-free wireless Bluetooth connection. One of the biggest challenges of using smartphones is to get users to realize they can do a lot more than make voice calls and exchange text messages. To a large degree, smartphones and tablets replace the need to carry a briefcase.

We've gone from text command line entry on typewriter-size keyboards to graphical touch screens and keyboards. 64GB SD memory cards the size of a fingernail, costing $30, have evolved from those $200 15-inch, 4MB disc platters. Internal memory has gone from 16KB of clunky core memory on the mini-computer based instruments to 16GB or more on today's PCs and mobile devices.

With Skype we have seen the end of expensive conference calling, the need to bill clients for long distance charges, and more importantly the ability to build businesses with worldwide human resource and customer bases at nominal cost. Hotels can no longer make money for long distance calls over landlines; at best they can charge fees for an Internet connection. Telephone booths have become museum pieces.

Phone numbers are masked behind names in calling directories. We are seeing the decline of landline calling but can now have free Group video calls around the world. One-to-one HD video calls on a large desktop screen make the other party look as if s/he is across the table; it's called telepresence. Fiber optic transmission lines allow us to watch television and videos from around the world—at no cost yet with excellent HD resolution. And almost every day I make overseas Skype calls but never see a bill.

So much for the history and my bio (you can find a more formal one on LinkedIn), it's time to get into the book and learn the complete story about using Skype and all its enriched communications features.

Chapter 1

People Like to Talk!

Whether you're a road warrior building business relationships, a parent catching up with the family's day, a grandparent watching your grandchildren grow, or whether you're simply keeping in touch with business colleagues and family members spread around the world, talk builds relationships and understanding through conversations. The challenge has always been the cost of bringing people together for a conversation when geographically separated.

In late August 2003, Skype™, a software application for making voice calls over the Internet, was launched. It was evolutionary in that it "just worked" for users who had a PC and Internet connection, yet it did not require a significant investment in capital equipment by Skype's founders. It was revolutionary in that making voice calls to anyone worldwide using this software was "free." Over the past 11 years "Skype" has evolved into a widely recognized brand, and a verb, describing how two or more parties communicate over the Internet.

From its beginnings offering voice calling and instant messaging, Skype 11 years later delivers over 36% of the world's international calling minutes, has brought video calling to the consumer and business masses, and has over 300 million monthly active users in over 180 countries. Its Group Chat facilitates ad hoc communications across business teams, special interest groups, and families. According to Skype, at least 40% of its users employ Skype for their business communications activities.

And Skype is everywhere. Its availability has spread from the PC to smartphones (such as the iPhone, Android phones, BlackBerry 10, and Windows Phone 8), tablets (such as iPad, Samsung Galaxy, and Surface Pro), TVs, and a range of other devices that offer real time voice, video, and/or text communications as a feature.

Most importantly it has opened up the world to low-cost or free conversations across a continent and over oceans. Multi-party calls allow families to have virtual reunions and businesses to take advantage of the best resources for a task without regard to location. While the informal grandparents call has been the biggest consumer application of video calling, Skype goes beyond the basic voice or video call to provide a rich conversation platform that builds and supports geographically dispersed collaborative business teams.

Why Skype?

There have been several applications available that provide chat, voice communications, and auxiliary features over the Internet. But with the rich combination of number of users worldwide, supported devices, three conversation modes, and high-quality and multi-party video, Skype's unique voice and video technology and low tariffs to call the telephone network worldwide have not been duplicated by any other offering.

Google supports real-time conversations but communications is not their primary focus; Apple FaceTime is limited to conversations between FaceTime-enabled Macs and other Apple devices; BBM offers excellent voice and video quality but can only be installed on one mobile device while mirrored to PCs and tablets; other offerings simply do not have the complete feature set of Skype.

Here's what makes Skype unique:

- The network effect[1]

    - Skype has as many as 40 to 86 million users online worldwide concurrently every day.

    - During June 2013 Skype reported that 299 million users had participated in at least one Skype conversation.

- In 2013 Skype-to-Skype calls represented 36%[2] of all international calling minutes according to Telegeography's annual survey.

---

[1]http://en.wikipedia.org/wiki/Network_effect
[2]http://www.telegeography.com/products/commsupdate/articles/2011/01/06/international-long-distance-slumps-while-skype-soars/

- In 2013, Skype international calling minutes grew 36%[3], while traditional carrier calling grew ~7%. (See Figure 1-1).

Increase in International Phone and Skype Traffic

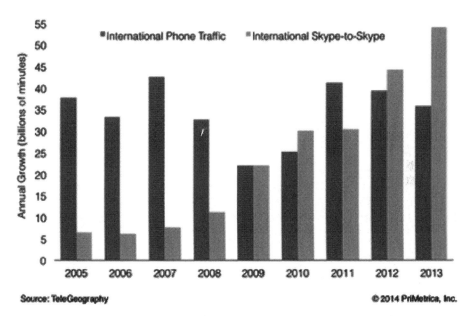

Figure 1-1. *Comparison of international phone and Skype traffic growth since 2005 (in minutes) (Source: Telegeography, http://www.telegeography.com/)*

- Skype supports, in a user friendly way, three modes of conversations: voice, chat, and video

- Skype everywhere: Placing and receiving Skype calls are supported on PCs, smartphones, tablets, Skype-enabled TVs, and gaming devices such as Xbox One. Calls can be made between any of these platforms.

- Skype is officially supported in 27 languages and 15 currencies.

- Skype provides support for calls to and from the legacy phone network at low tariffs worldwide.

[3]http://www.telegeography.com/press/press-releases/2012/01/09/international-call-traffic-growth-slows-as-skypes-volumes-soar/index.html

- ▩ Skype provides cost effective subscriptions for effectively unlimited calling to as many as 61 countries.

- ▩ Skype provides support for multi-party voice conversations with up to 25 participants. Group chats can support up to 300 participants.

- ▩ Skype introduced its multi-party Group Video Calling in early 2011, supporting multi-party video calls with up to ten participants. In early 2014, Skype announced that Group Video Calling would become a free service.

- ▩ Skype for TV supports select Internet-enabled LG, Panasonic, Philips, Samsung, Sharp, Sony, Toshiba, and Vizio TVs, as well as select Panasonic and Sony Blu-ray players and the TelyHD Skype for TV webcam as end point terminals for originating and receiving Skype calls.

- ▩ Skype provides a contact directory and enriches conversations through presence information, file transfer, SMS messaging, call forwarding, multi-party conversations, PC desktop sharing, voice mail, video messaging, and basic text conversation archiving.

About 40% of all active Skype users sign in to Skype daily. Obviously free Skype-to-Skype voice and video calling dominates usage. While no real statistics exist, probably 90% of those minutes involve calls that simply would not be made (or last as long) if there were charges associated with the calls. And it confirms that video calling has become a major feature encouraging Skype adoption and usage.

In summary, Skype has become a universal brand name, and even a verb, associated with making free or low cost calls over the Internet. It's a name that does not even require translation in many languages.

Most important is the wide range of Skype user experiences. Skype overcomes geographical barriers while enhancing business productivity. Building collaborative business teams, carrying out job interviews, enhancing customer support operations and supporting remote training and education all contribute to the business case for using Skype. On the personal side Skype facilitates romances, helps in natural disasters, keeps family members in touch, supports learning a new language and, due to its crystal clear audio, is used for teaching music. Skype video calling resulted in the mass adoption of the video calling concept first demonstrated in AT&T's picture phone exhibit at the 1964 World's Fair[4]; today video is used in over 40% of Skype calls.

---

[4]http://en.wikipedia.org/wiki/Videophone#AT.26T_Picturephone

WHY DID SKYPE TAKE OFF IN 2003?

While many attempts had been made to launch Internet-based voice calling applications in the late 1990s and early 2000s none had really been adopted due to issues with the Internet infrastructure, including service speeds, security, and the lack of a file sharing architecture called peer-to-peer sharing. The processing power of PCs had been too slow to effectively handle voice calling as one application amongst several running concurrently.

As a result at Skype's launch time (late August 2003) the underlying market conditions and technology foundation had converged to set the stage for rapid acceptance and adoption of Skype in the fall of 2003.

From a presentation by Skype at eComm 2008:

- IP-based audio technology that could support real time conversations had matured.

- Multimedia PCs became the standard, incorporating higher speed processors and the requisite audio hardware–microphones and speakers.

- Broadband (cable and DSL) Internet services had become widely available worldwide.

- Technology for dealing with firewalls associated with consumer routers had been developed.

- Instant Messaging networks had become widely accepted.

- A robust and scalable peer-to-peer file sharing infrastructure had been developed and widely adopted for other applications (especially in Skype's founders' previous ventures).

So the stage had been set; over 99% of the solution for a robust, reliable, secure, and high-quality real time communications platform was in place.

Skype launched the appropriate software application with the right formula. Its ease of installation, along with the abilities to place "free" voice calls with one click, build a contact directory, and complement voice with instant messaging combined to make Skype calls a winning user experience. Within the first month after launch, Skype had over 500,000 downloads. At the time of writing this book over 800 million Skype accounts have been created, with over 300 million monthly active users.

The rest, as they say, is history.

What Is Skype?

Skype is a software program that is very easy to install, and it's easy to set up an account, find contacts, and start calling. Skype is one of the more robust software applications on Windows and Mac platforms. Skype has matured to the point where it can readily seek out and identify the hardware it needs to support a conversation: a microphone, speakers and, for video calls, a webcam. The path to making that first Skype call is almost frictionless.

Skype calls can also be made to or from many mobile phones. A carrier-agnostic Skype client is available for phones and tablets supported by iOS (iPhone, iPad, and iPod Touch), Android, BlackBerry 10 phones and, most recently, Windows Phone 8 and Amazon Fire.

Skype is also available on certain models of LG, Panasonic, Philips, Samsung, Sharp, Sony, Toshiba and Vizio TVs, as well as Panasonic and Sony Blu-ray players. Skype is also available for making and receiving Skype calls on any HDTV using the intelligent TelyHD webcam.

Beyond free Skype-to-Skype voice and video calls and chat, Skype supports low cost voice calls to conventional landlines and mobile phones worldwide (PSTN) as well as SMS messaging. Skype also offers online numbers that allow calls from the PSTN to be made to a user's Skype on a PC, smartphone, or TV. Skype To Go is a service, available in 24 countries, that lets you make calls to any landline worldwide (and mobiles in Canada/U.S. and six other countries) at Skype rates by calling local numbers.

In many ways, think of Skype as a worldwide uberplatform for conversation that allows you to make calls worldwide independently from the legacy phone companies.

A major key to Skype's wide adoption and acceptance is its Skype Everywhere initiative (see Figure 1-2). Skype calls can be made between any Skype-enabled devices, such as from a mobile smartphone to a TV, from a Mac to a Windows PC, between an iPhone and an Android phone, or between an iPhone and a Windows PC.

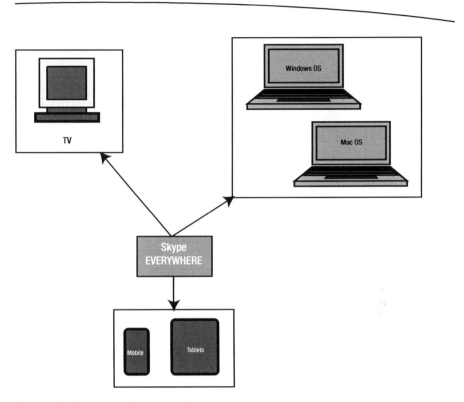

Figure 1-2. Skype is platform agnostic

In September, 2011 Skype released upgrades to all its PC and mobile clients which introduced advertising on free Skype-to-Skype calls. However, if you have Skype credit or a Skype Calling Plan subscription, you will not see the advertising.

In November 2014 Microsoft announced that its enterprise grade communications platform, Microsoft Lync, would be rebranded in 2015. In fact Skype for Business will adopt many of the user interface features discussed in this book. Microsoft Lync, as it exists in late 2014 with instant messaging and voice connectivity to Skype, will be discussed in Chapter 12.

However, the original Skype, covered in this book, will continue to be available as a low cost alternative that can continue to provide cost and productivity benefits to business users who want to build a worldwide business ecosystem.

Where and When Do You Use Skype?

With Skype available on so many platforms, it is worth spending a few minutes looking at why Skype is used on each of the various platforms with a focus on PCs, smartphones, tablets, and TVs.

Skype on PCs

Skype for Windows desktop continues to have the most complete feature set for enriching Skype conversations; Skype for Mac has become fairly ubiquitous with the increasing popularity of MacBooks and iMacs. These versions of Skype can be used anywhere that one has a Windows PC or Mac, whether at home, in the office or while traveling with a laptop. Figure 1-3 gives an overview of the features available when using Skype on a PC.

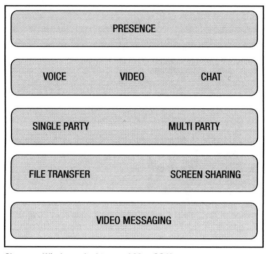

Skype on Windows desktop and Mac OS X

Figure 1-3. Feature set of Skype on Windows desktop or Mac OS X

In November 2011 Skype released, concurrently, versions of Skype for Windows and Skype for Mac that for the first time supported the same major feature set on both clients although the user interface experience continued to be somewhat different.

In the fall of 2012 Skype introduced Skype for Windows 8 or 'modern Windows', a second version available for use with Windows 8.x PCs and tablets. While it can be accessed on desktop and laptop PCs using Windows 8.1, this version is designed also to work with touch screen Windows tablets, such as Microsoft's Surface Pro and various OEM vendors of Windows 8 tablets. Its feature set has gradually been enhanced to include many of the features of Skype for Windows desktop; however, there is no long term archiving and search capability.

Beyond one-to-one conversations, on PCs you can:

- Host group chats as well as voice and video multi-party calls.

- Administer group chat sessions for collaboration: business teams and special interest groups make heavy use of Skype's persistent group chat feature.

- Maintain in the chat session pane not only an ongoing ad hoc dialogue, but also meeting agendas and notes, shared URLs, file transfer information, and ad hoc "water fountain" discussions.

- Log all voice and video conversation activity, including what is known in the communications business as call detail records with the time and length of individual calls.

- Log all activity in the session that occurs on any mobile device following the same chat session.

- Archive chat discussions for later recall; the author has two group chat sessions that have run continuously for over seven years.

- Search the archives for key words or phrases going back to the beginning of the group chat session.

- Participate in multiple (Group) Chat sessions on a single screen; one company has over 20 concurrent group chats for various purposes.

- Connect to Facebook to follow Facebook news feeds in the Skype client's Home View and also participate in Facebook Messenger chat sessions.

While Skype for Windows desktop has the most complete Skype feature set, Skype for Mac supports most of those features. However, there are significant differences in how the two Skype clients operate and access those features as discussed in Chapter 5. On Windows 8 PCs with two versions available, Skype for Windows desktop remains the preferred version for business use due to its support of archiving and search and more intuitive user interface.

Skype on Smartphones and Tablets

The dream Skype experience, especially with the launch of the iPhone in 2008, includes the ability to make and receive calls worldwide at no cost from mobile smartphones and tablets. Now supported on iOS, Android, BlackBerry 10, Windows Phone 8, Windows 8 tablets, and Amazon Fire tablets—including video calling and video messaging—Skype conversations over mobile are becoming a significant portion of Skype traffic. This has added significantly to the possible use cases for Skype. Figure 1-4 gives an overview of the features available when using Skype on a mobile device.

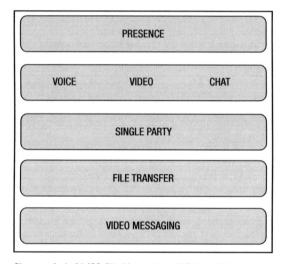

Skype on Android, iOS, Blackberry 10 and Windows Phone 8

Figure 1-4. Feature set of Skype on smartphones

With Skype apps on smartphones and tablets, you can take your conversation with you. While not at the point where calls can be automatically switched between a PC and smartphone, you can continue to follow chat sessions, including group chats, while away from your PC, participate in group calls, place and receive Skype-to-Skype calls, place calls to landlines and mobile phones and receive calls at a Skype Online number. It complements your PC-based calling when away from the home or office.

In September 2014 Skype started rolling out the ability to host multi-party voice calls on a smartphone or tablet. Initially available on the iPhone 5 or later for calls with up to four participants, this feature will probably migrate to other smartphones and tablets over the next few months. In the meantime, a smartphone or tablet user can participate in a multi-party voice or video call.

But there are some issues with this:

- The biggest one is battery drain; the combination of using a Wi-Fi access point and Skype on a mobile smartphone accelerates battery drain. Skype has recently made significant improvements to reduce battery drain, but it still places an additional load on the battery.

- Skype calls involving iPhone, Android, BlackBerry 10, or Windows Phone 8, whether Skype-to-Skype or outbound calling to the phone network, use a wireless carrier's data plans when using 3G/LTE services. Ensure you have a multi-gigabyte monthly data plan if you plan on doing a lot of calling over your home carrier.

- You will want to limit your Skype calling on smartphones to Wi-Fi connections only while roaming on foreign carriers. Roaming charges for data services at 10-20 MB per 10 minutes of calling could drain your bank account. Precautionary measures to consider when roaming are discussed in Chapter 6. When nothing else is available, Skype Wi-Fi can provide a connection at about $0.25 per minute.

- Skype on a mobile device only archives activity going back 30 days; also there is no archive Search capability.

Skype for TV

At CES 2010 Skype announced Skype for TV where Skype software is embedded into Internet-enabled TV sets from Samsung and Panasonic. Today Skype for TV is available on LG, Panasonic, Philips, Samsung, Sharp, Sony, Toshiba, and Vizio as well as Panasonic and Sony Blu-ray players. At CES 2012 TelyLabs introduced TelyHD, the first device designed to bring Skype calling to any HDTV.

Initially available on high-end HDTVs, Skype is now being supported on many lower cost "smart" HDTV models.

However, Skype for TV sessions cannot be participants in group voice or video calls. Later in the book I talk about using Skype on a TV panel in a conference room.

Skype as a Business and Productivity Tool

Beyond making free voice calls, Skype enhances calls with its features that provide tools for sharing documents, facilitating group collaboration, keeping conversation notes, leaving messages, and holding virtual meetings. In summary, Skype is a productivity tool that facilitates business processes across geographies, minimizes friction, and reduces both communications and travel costs. It allows a business to operate more effectively and efficiently.

So which Skype client do I use in a business setting? The key questions to ask include:

▧ How many of the unique features, such as persistent conversation log archiving, on desktop and laptop PCs would be used?

▧ How much physical desktop footprint is desired?

▧ Will video calling, including group video calling, be used?

▧ What is required for the road warrior or when outside the home office?

▧ Is it necessary to follow Skype activity both at the home office and on the road?

Using Skype In the Office

When in the office, you can use Skype as the primary business desktop phone, placing and receiving calls over Skype or the legacy phone network. On any PC or mobile device the Skype application can receive calls from the legacy phone network using a Skype Online number. As a result there are cases where office workers only can be contacted on Skype. On the other hand a feature called SIP Connect, discussed later, allows a Skype user to effectively become an extension of a business PBX.

A desktop or laptop PC has the advantage of allowing you to use a regular PC keyboard for chat sessions, which is especially useful if you are typing long messages. The desktop or laptop screen size also allows flexibility over how Skype is displayed such that one can, say, follow multiple chat sessions in separate windows or, in a board room setting, allow (group) video calls to be followed on a large screen display, such as a TV monitor.

Skype for iPad, or larger Android tablets, however, provides some unique opportunities in the office where it can become a "default" video phone. In this role, a tablet can replace the legacy desktop phone while maintaining a small footprint and its independence from a PC. Its screen size makes it ideal for following a video call without placing demand on the resources of a PC; it can also serve as a speaker phone in a small office. With its much higher capacity battery, battery drain is not a significant issue.

Using Skype On the Road

While travelling, you have the choice of three platforms: laptops with the complete Skype feature set, smartphones with a small display, or tablets with a larger display. The latter two support basic chat, voice, and video conversations, usually via a touch display and keyboard, but are limited with respect to group calling and archiving conversation activity.

A Skype account can be open concurrently on multiple platforms; each device will mirror activity to the other PCs and devices logged in to the same account. At the most basic level, these mobile devices allow the user to walk out of her home office and continue to participate in conversations.

On the other hand, smartphones and tablets:

- Provide a lightweight and small profile platform for following Skype.

- Require Internet access via a carrier or Wi-Fi; more details will be discussed in Chapter 2.

- Should be recharged at least daily to ensure availability throughout the day.

Since the Microsoft acquisition of Skype in late 2011, significant effort has been made to improve both the feature set and robustness of Skype on mobile devices. A major example is the increase in video resolution supported from a grainy 160x120 image to a very clear HD-quality resolution. Features added include video messaging, file transfer (photos only on iOS devices), and a common user interface across all devices.

On all mobile devices, Skype can be available in the background and provide notifications of new activity. Skype on iPhone and BlackBerry 10 support Bluetooth connection to an automobile's audio system. Bluetooth connectivity is not supported on Android and Windows Phone devices due to the multiple hardware platforms supported.

> **Caution**   iPhone and BlackBerry 10 support the Bluetooth audio connection to car audio in a "hands-free" manner. However, to launch a call or do any text chat pull over to the side of the road to carry out activities that require using the device's touch screen or hardware keyboard. Many jurisdictions now have "distracted driving" legislation with stiff penalties. Even more importantly, statistics show that distracted driving now accounts for as many accidents and fatalities as driving under the influence of alcohol and/or drugs.

Where Does This Book Take You?

This book is intended to be a guide and tutorial on using Skype in a business setting. Going forward:

- Chapter 2 covers getting started with Skype and making connections to the Internet.

- Chapter 3 provides a more detailed discussion of how Skype can enrich conversations through sharing activities, logging, and archiving.

- Chapter 4 talks about some use cases where Skype has helped a business grow, both internally across geographically dispersed business teams and externally into expanded market opportunities worldwide.

- Chapter 5 goes into details about using Skype on PCs (Windows desktop and Mac OS X).

- Chapter 6 covers how Skype works on mobile smartphones and tablets.

- Chapter 7 provides information on making and receiving calls to and from landlines and mobile phones.

- Chapter 8 goes into why chat can become an ongoing relationship and team building tool for a business team.

- Chapter 9 reviews how to manage your Skype account and make payments for PSTN-connected calls.

- Chapter 10 summarizes the hardware considerations for using Skype.

- Chapter 11 talks about using Skype as a team collaboration tool.

- Chapter 12 discusses how Skype has been integrated into other Microsoft products such as Outlook, Outlook.com, and Microsoft Lync.

- Chapter 13 takes a look at what we can expect from IP-based (i.e. Internet) communications going forward.

- Appendix A provides a glossary describing terminology and protocols, such as VoIP and PSTN, associated with using Skype and other IP-based communication tools.

Summary

The bottom line is that your Skype activity can be personalized to your mix of business and personal communications activities, whether in the home office or on the road. You have options to remain connected either in real time or, for chat, asynchronously. With its presence and notification options you can set priorities for which calls require immediate attention, which are call forwarded to another Skype account or phone number, and which should be sent to voice/video messaging.

Key Points

- Skype is a universal communications application that facilitates worldwide communications and overcomes geographical barriers.

- Skype has the most complete feature set of over-the-top Internet-based communications offerings.

- Skype is virtually platform agnostic, available on all PCs, smartphones, and tablets commonly used in business or at home.

- Skype enriches voice and video communications through features such as file transfer, screen sharing, video messaging, and conversation archiving and search.

- Skype supports business team collaboration beyond one-to-one conversations through its multi-party group chat, voice, and video features.

■ Skype continues to be the fastest growing communications service provider worldwide.

■ With its support of video calling, Skype is ideal for business presentations, negotiations and virtual meetings (especially international calls) as well as the "friends and family" calls.

■ And, as your primary business phone, it goes with you when you leave the office but have Skype available on a laptop PC, iPhone, iPad, Android, BlackBerry 10, or Windows Phone 8.

Chapter 2

Connecting to Skype at Home and Abroad

Besides a robust Internet connection, you will need to install a Skype client or app and create a Skype account (with an associated Skype profile).

A key feature of Skype is that it provides direct (or peer-to-peer) voice and video connections between Skype call participants over the Internet, bypassing the legacy phone communications networks. Skype converts your audio into digital packets assigned a unique identifier; these packets are then transmitted over the Internet to the other party (or participants) on the call. At the other party's end, these packets are then converted back into a crystal clear audio signal that can be heard on a headset or speakers. And it's only because the processors on PCs and mobile devices have become so powerful that all this conversion activity can happen in real time.

However, also critical to using Skype is the availability of a robust Internet connection, whether via wired Ethernet connected to a PC or wirelessly over Wi-Fi or a wireless carrier's data plan. The key parameters related to Skype use are download speed and, for video, upload speed, especially as video resolution and the number of participants in a group video call increases. Minimum and recommended speeds increase as you goes from chat to voice to standard resolution video to HD video. Hosting group voice and, especially, group video also require increasingly faster connections for the host connection only.

When connecting to Skype at home or abroad, it is often important to know that your communications are private and that your connection is secure, especially if you are discussing sensitive business information, so this is the final topic covered in this chapter. First, let's talk about establishing a Skype account, incorporating a Skype profile, connecting to the Internet, and then we'll cover building a Contact directory.

Opening a Skype Account

Prior to making calls you must create and open a Skype account. The Skype software is downloaded for installation as follows:

- For PCs, go to www.skype.com in any browser and select Downloads; the default Skype client for your particular Windows PC or Mac is offered for download.

- For mobile devices, go to the relevant app store (Apple App Store, Google Play, BlackBerry World, Windows Store, or Amazon Appstore) and install the Skype application.

Opening the application brings up a login screen (Figure 2-1) with options for creating a Skype account using a unique Skype name or your Microsoft account if you have one (this option also applies to non-Windows devices). On Windows PCs and Macs you may also create an account using your Facebook login email and password.

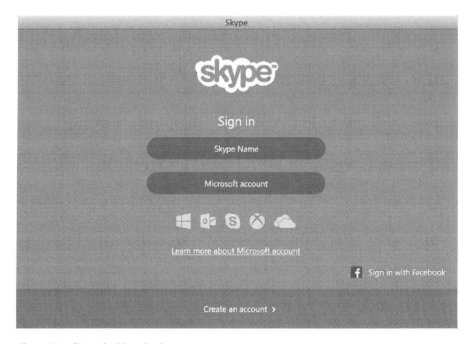

Figure 2-1. Skype for Mac sign in screen

Another option is to go to the Skype website (www.skype.com), select Sign In, and there will be an opportunity to create a Skype account and provide Profile information.

When creating a Skype account there are two required items:

- Skype Name: When you install Skype and register as a Skype user you create a unique Skype Name or SkypeID. Think carefully about your selection as it can never be changed (and becomes your unique, permanently assigned identification as a Skype user).

- Email address: At registration you must enter at least one email address to associate with your Skype Name. Later you can add two more email addresses to associate with the same Skype Name. You can always change the associated email address(es).

From your Skype account manager on the Skype website you can also associate (or merge) your Skype Account with your Microsoft account and log in via either. This is important for Windows 8 users, especially on Windows 8.1 tablets, as the login to Windows 8 automatically logs you in to the Skype app on the modern Windows interface.

> **Note**   Your initial account is a Personal Skype account, owned and managed by you as an individual. Skype Manager, discussed later in this book, allows a business administrator to establish and manage Business Skype accounts. These accounts are owned by a business for use by individual employees, as well as for multi-user devices such as PBXs that incorporate Skype connections.
>
> If you plan to make your Skype account accessible with Microsoft Lync, which is an enterprise grade communications Microsoft platform discussed in Chapter 12, you must log in to your Skype account using your Microsoft login.

The Home Screen

On logging in to Skype, the Home Screen appears. Common to all devices are the terms Recent, Favorites, and People. On mobile devices and Skype for modern Windows this appears as shown in Figure 2-2.

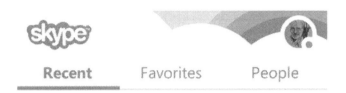

Figure 2-2. The Skype Home screen header

On Windows Desktop and Mac OS X the term Contacts remains in use while Recent and Favorites appear with Contacts in the left pane (see Figure 2-3).

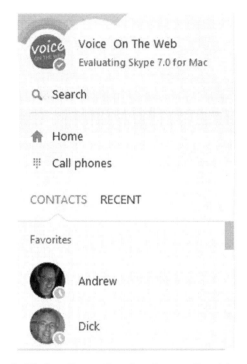

Figure 2-3. The Skype for Windows Recent, Favorites, Contacts (People) configuration

Building a Skype Profile

When registering an account, Skype creates a Skype Profile containing as little or as much information about yourself and how to contact you as you choose (Figure 2-4).

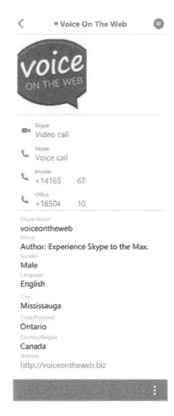

Figure 2-4. A Skype Profile on Android/BlackBerry 10

There are three ways to access your Skype Profile:

■ In the Windows or Mac client, click your own name in the top-left corner.

■ For mobile, tap on your Skype Profile image in the upper right of the Home screen, tap on the Account image to change the image, and select My Account | Profile or View Profile to add/change other profile information.

■ Log into your Skype account at www.skype.com.

After creating an account you will want to build your Skype Profile, which can include:

- **Your Profile picture:** This can be a photograph (with an option to take a picture with a webcam or mobile device camera) or a graphics file. This is probably the most significant personal branding associated with your Skype activity.

- **Email address:** One is required; up to two more optional.

- **Landline and mobile phone numbers (optional):** Office, home, and mobile

- **Your "home base" location:** Optional as to the level of detail. You can enter city, state/province, country.

- **A website URL:** Useful for promoting a blog or business.

- **Birthdate:** Optional, but you will get lots of birthday greetings if you enter this.

- **Language:** Skype supports over 25 languages.

- **Time:** (with an option to use the PC's clock or mobile device's clock). Important if you do a lot of calling across time zones. This lets your contacts see what your local time is.

- **About me:** Here you can enter any information you choose. For instance, you might specify your criteria for acceptance of others as one of your Contacts. Other uses include identifying your activities–either personal or work.

Profile Considerations

The Profile Picture can be either a stored image or from your webcam. This image, which brands your Skype activity, is displayed:

- In your own Profile (where you can change it, if desired)

- In your Contacts' People/Contact lists

- On call screens during a call (if not using video)–including multi-party calls

- In View Profile windows when selected by your Contacts in their Skype clients

- Optionally, in Skype 7 for Windows/Mac, conversation screens beside every message you enter

Your Profile Picture also shows up in the "as Pictures" View of Skype for Mac.

Entering a mobile phone number is important for two reasons:

- You can receive SMS messages sent from other Skype contacts' Skype chat windows on your mobile phone. (More details on sending SMS messages are in Chapter 6.)

- This can serve as your Skype CallerID for outbound calls to landlines and mobile phones.

An important consideration is that your time zone is set correctly and displays to your accepted contacts (Figure 2-5). When working across time zones, it's often helpful to know the contact's local time prior to making a voice or video call. Synchronizing with your local PC's time (My computer's setting) ensures your time is correct when traveling.

Figure 2-5. Time zone examples

The settings that you establish in the Profile screen (Figure 2-6) are carried across to any Skype client you may open on another PC (Windows or Mac) and Skype for iPhone/Android/iPad/BlackBerry/Windows Phone. If you make changes on the other devices, they will change the profile settings seen on this screen.

Figure 2-6. Skype Profile as viewed by contacts

Now let's turn to the various ways to connect with Skype over the Internet.

Connecting to Skype at Home and Abroad

Having a Skype account established, including a Profile, the other major requirement is a suitable Internet connection. While in the early days, wired connections were the norm at home or the home office, today wireless connections, whether over Wi-Fi at home, on the road, or via a wireless carrier have become the predominant Internet access connection.

Home Office

Skype requires a standard business or residence Internet service plan. These usually incorporate a cable modem/router that provides both wired Ethernet and Wi-Fi connectivity.

Fortunately, business and residence services have made significant Internet speed increases. Most high-speed services under user-controlled subscriptions (>10Mbps download and >2Mbps upload) are sufficient for Skype activity. This is especially true for services using fiber or cable (which in practice may be a hybrid fiber/cable connection).

> **Note** To test Internet download/upload speeds use a service such as Speedtest.net. An example speed test is shown in Figure 2-7.

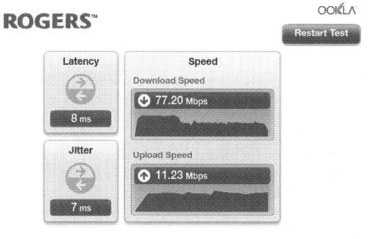

Figure 2-7. Speed test on a 60Mpbs/download, 10MBps upload hybrid cable service

> **Note** Another consideration is the home or office local area network router along with firewalls. One reason for Skype's widespread adoption is that it transparently addresses most of the issues related to passing through a router and firewalls available as a component of the most popular security software. However, Skype does have a support page for rare instances where issues such as proxy servers and firewalls must be considered (see https://support.skype.com/en/search?q=firewalls).

A table of minimum and recommended Internet bandwidth speeds for chat, voice, and video is in the Glossary of this book.

Accessing the Internet wirelessly, especially when away from the home office or home where the user must use a wireless carrier's data plan or a publicly accessible Wi-Fi connection, can be a challenge for a variety of reasons.

Public Wi-Fi

Publicly accessible Wi-Fi connections are becoming more readily available in airports, restaurants, coffee shops, hotels, hospitals and medical centers, conference centers, highway service centers, cruise ships, and other locations. However, the speed and quality of service may vary considerably.

■ Wi-Fi in locations where there is the potential to be a large number of users may be compromised if too many hotel guests or conference attendees are attempting to use the same core Internet connection at the same time at the hosting location. Indications are slow download speeds, intermittent access, or even an inability to access the service.

■ Some locations offer free services (that can tend to have lower capacity and speeds) while others charge for a service, either for basic access or, especially at hotels, for a premium service offering higher speeds.

■ Security can be an issue, especially when offered by generic names, such as free or simply don't require a login or Wi-Fi password. On the other hand many "brand name" locations provide appropriate levels of security to minimize the opportunity for a compromised connection.

SKYPE WIFI

Normally Skype connections are made through wired and wireless connections available at various remote locations. In particular, Wi-Fi connections depend on the availability of a readily available Wi-Fi Internet service and/or subscription, such as Boingo, or a free service, such as is available at Starbucks in U.S. and Canada. Some hotels and airports, especially outside the U.S. and Canada, have high hourly or daily Internet charges.

However, for the occasions when there is no alternative, Skype provides Skype WiFi[1], working with Wi-Fi service providers worldwide[2] to provision over 2 million access points.

If you end up in a location supported by Skype WiFi, your Skype client on a Wi-Fi–enabled Windows or Mac PC, or the Skype WiFi application for mobile devices, will recognize its availability through a pop-up window. It then offers the opportunity to use Skype WiFi.

---

[1]http://www.skype.com/intl/en-us/features/allfeatures/skype-access/
[2]http://about.skype.com/press/2011/02/wifi.html

Payment is through Skype credit. The Skype WiFi price per minute varies by provider and is displayed when you connect to a compatible Wi-Fi hotspot.

Per minute rates of 15 cents to 50 cents per minute (or more or less depending on the access point service) are not exactly the lowest but Skype WiFi is a service of convenience not intended for long term use (as you might do at a free Wi-Fi coffee shop).

Skype-to-Skype calls via Skype WiFi are still at no additional charge; SkypeOut calls require either a Skype Calling Plan subscription or Skype credit in addition to the Skype WiFi charge.

Of course, with a Skype WiFi Internet connection, you can also check email, Twitter and Facebook, browse the web, and run all your other Internet-enabled applications.

Wireless Carriers

Using Skype on a smartphone or tablet over a wireless carrier requires a data plan; on your home carrier a multi-GB data plan subscription is recommended. It is wise to check your usage frequently; also be aware of overage charges for going over your carrier's plan limits.

However roaming charges on "foreign" wireless carriers can drain your wallet very quickly. Four solutions to this are

- Place the phone in Airplane (iPhone, iPad, BlackBerry 10) or Flight (Android) mode, while leaving Wi-Fi on (Figure 2-8). As discussed earlier in this chapter, Wi-Fi access points are becoming more and more prevalent to the point where they are becoming the Stealth carrier[3].

Figure 2-8. Airplane mode

---

[3]http://voiceontheweb.biz/2010/02/reprise-is-wifi-becoming-the-unregulated-stealth-carrier-of-the-future/

■ Most smartphones also have a setting to automatically turn off data when roaming.

　■ On iPhone go to Settings ➤ Cellular ➤ Data Roaming.

　■ On BlackBerry 10 go to Settings ➤ Mobile Network ➤ Data Services.

　■ On Android go to Settings ➤ More Settings ➤ Flight Mode or ➤ Airplane Mode (hardware dependent)

■ Purchase roaming packages from the home carrier; while still relatively expensive they tend not to be as expensive as pay-as-you-go roaming.

■ Use a multi-country SIM, such as Truphone's with a World Plan that provides voice, SMS, and data connections in up to 66 countries under a single multi-country plan

Making Skype voice calls on a carrier requires at least a 3G connection. In many cases, especially in rural areas, there may be only a 2G/EDGE or even no carrier connection. Ensure you have at least a 3G connection for voice; having a HSPA or LTE connection will enhance the quality of video calls. The carrier connection status usually shows up in the top bar of the home screen of a smartphone. A typical example is shown in Figure 2-9.

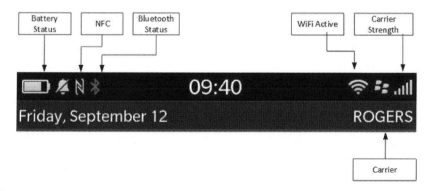

Figure 2-9. *Carrier and Wi-Fi connection indicators: In this case an LTE connection is shown (what we recognize as the standard Wi-Fi symbol) but it could show 3, H, 2 or E for 3G, HSPA, 2G or EDGE*

Managing Contacts: Whom Are You Going to Call?

The key parameter for any communications offering is the number of users; this, in turn, determines how many contacts you can accumulate. Today with over 300 million monthly active Skype users, the chances of a business colleague, friend, or family member having an active Skype account is very high.

Contacts can be divided into

- Skype contacts, with whom you can hold Skype-to-Skype chat, voice, and video conversations.

- Phone contacts with whom you can hold voice conversations only.

While you must initially establish a "contact relationship" with Skype contacts (described in the next section), phone contacts come from several sources, including:

- A Skype contact's Skype profile, which can include up to three phone numbers (Home, Work, Mobile)

- From Windows PCs and devices, Outlook's People contacts containing phone numbers.

- On mobile devices and Macs, the native Contacts directory

- Facebook friends whose About information includes phone numbers

- Manual entry using the dial pad

A COMMENT ABOUT EMAIL ADDRESSES REGISTERED WITH SKYPE

While you must associate your Skype account with at least one email address (and, optionally, up to three), Skype does not make email addresses publicly available, including disclosure in any Skype User Profile that can be viewed publicly. Skype uses email addresses to:

- Allow a response to a user's search for a Skype contact, provided the user knows your email address through other sources, such as through private communications or via a search of a user's address book(s) in Outlook or Facebook. This is available via Skype for Windows Import Contacts feature.

- Send emails confirming your purchase of Skype Credit or a Skype subscription, or of Skype Manager activity.

- Send emails related to compensation for outages or other service disruptions when Skype, at its sole discretion, decides to offer compensation.

Skype will never send emails requesting your login information (password) or credit card information or emails creating a false sense of urgency.

Skype Contacts

Upon creating an account, the first activity is to build up a Skype People (or Contacts) directory for the account. You can search for contacts (Figure 2-10) using one of the following: a full name, an email address, a Skype name or, in the case of Android or BlackBerry 10, a phone number (including country code).

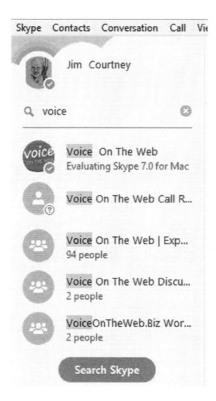

Figure 2-10. Skype for Windows contact search

Note   While traditionally called Contacts in Skype, Microsoft has decided to change the name for all their contact directories (including Outlook 2013) to "People". This term appears in Skype for mobile devices and Skype for Windows 8 Modern.

Preferred are searches for an email address or a Skype name as these tend to be unique to a single person. A user may include up to three email addresses on his/her Skype profile. The phone number search requires that a user has included one or more phone numbers in his/her Skype profile. Unless a user has included home location information, searching for a full name can bring up many users with similar names for selection–at this point location information helps narrow the choices.

When you select a prospective contact, Skype sends a chat message to the contact requesting permission to establish an ongoing Skype Contact relationship (Figure 2-11).

Figure 2-11. Requesting contact relationship

Note   Once a Skype Contact relationship has been established, that person (and his/her public profile information) will be available under People (or Contacts) on Skype on any PC or mobile device logged in to the same Skype account.

But there are some very important caveats in order to protect your privacy and prevent spamming:

- You need to know a Contact's email address or Skype name from other sources. Skype does not display email addresses when viewing a Contact's Skype Profile or make any suggestions when entering an email address into the Add a Contact form. Once entered into a Search box, Skype simply indicates its validity as an email address that has been registered with a Skype account.

- Initially you are sending out an invitation to become a contact. The recipient of the invitation needs to respond to your request via an Allow button that appears on their Skype client; he or she also has an option to Reject an invitation or Block a Contact from trying again.

- If an invitation is blocked, there is also an option to report the inviting contact for abuse. If Skype receives several abuse reports associated with a contact, it will investigate and, where appropriate, close down the account.

Selecting Favorites

As you build up contacts under People, you will find that there are some contacts with whom you have frequent conversations–business colleagues, customers, and suppliers along with family members and friends (Figure 2-12). Skype includes a Favorites feature to provide ready access to those contacts. Simply find the contact under People (Contacts) and designate it as a Favorite:

- **On Windows Desktop PCs and Macs:** Find the contact, right-click and select Add to Favorites or drag the Contact up to the Favorites section of the directory.

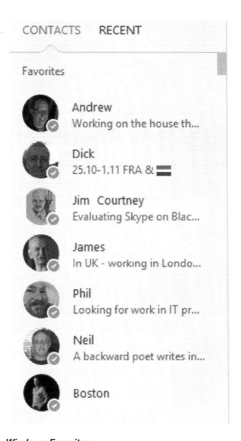

Figure 2-12. Skype for Windows Favorites

■ **On mobile devices:** Locate the contact under People, tap the contact name to bring up the chat conversation screen and then tap the three dot menu in the lower or upper right, and select Add to Favorites (Figure 2-13).

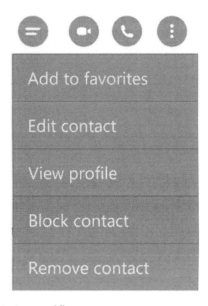

Figure 2-13. Manage contacts on mobile

■ **On Android and BlackBerry (alternate):** Locate the contact under People, tap and hold the contact name until a menu appears, and select Add to Favorites.

While Skype user profiles and the associated information appear in People or Contacts whenever you log in to an account on any device, Favorites are currently local device specific. In other words, you must create a separate set of Favorites for each device where an account is logged in.

When viewing People, the contacts can be filtered via a drop-down menu (Figure 2-14) to view All, Skype, Online/Available, or Facebook (Windows PCs and Macs only). Skype includes all Skype Contacts while Online/Available includes only those Contacts who are currently logged into Skype. On Skype for Windows Desktop simply go to Contacts ➤ Contact Lists; on Skype for Mac OS X the filtering options appear at the top of the Contacts screen.

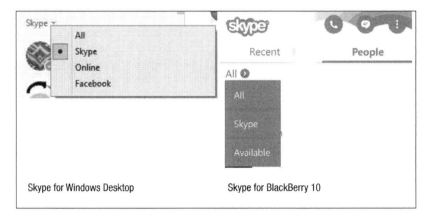

Figure 2-14. *Contact filters*

Within Skype for Windows Desktop and Skype for Mac OS X there is also a search box that supports a search for an individual contact. Effectively Favorites is a proxy for searching out frequently called Contacts on mobile devices.

Contact Status

One of the significant benefits of Skype is the ability to display Contact Status. To display this status on PC's, click the indicator in the lower-right corner of your Skype Profile image in the name pane to select a drop-down menu and select a status (Figure 2-15). On mobile devices, from the Home Page, tap on your Skype Profile image to see/select your status.

Figure 2-15. *Skype Status Options*

Online is the automatic default when you launch Skype on a PC; however, after several (designated) minutes of inactivity on your PC your status changes to Away. Other options for more privacy include Do Not Disturb, Invisible (not seen by other Contacts), and Offline (usually when either you are not logged in to Skype or you have lost the Internet connection).

With the exception of iPhone/iPad, Skype on mobile devices and modern Windows often only provide two status options: Available and Invisible (incorporating Do Not Disturb, Offline, and Away).

> **Note**   In Skype for Windows Desktop, if you hover over a Contact's name in either Contacts or Recent you will see a small dialog box that provides not only the Contact's name but also when they were last active on Skype (whether Online or Offline).

In the next section, we discuss Skype's security provisions and the options available for managing your privacy.

Skype Security and Privacy

Since launch, Skype voice and chat conversations are highly encrypted, providing a significant degree of confidentiality for your Skype conversations. In fact, security agencies are frustrated due to the level of security as they cannot readily "wiretap" into Skype-to-Skype calls.

Skype's security and privacy policies (`http://www.skype.com/intl/en-us/security/online-safety/`) and their execution address not only issues related to the content of conversations but also identity theft, phishing, and other online safety issues. Within Skype's options you can also limit who can contact you and launch conversations with you to, say, people whom you have accepted as contacts.

Skype Privacy Settings

In Skype for Windows, Tools | Options | Privacy allows you to set who you want to receive calls from, who is to know you have video capability, and other settings related to your overall privacy (see Figure 2-16). It is recommended you review these settings when initially setting up Skype.

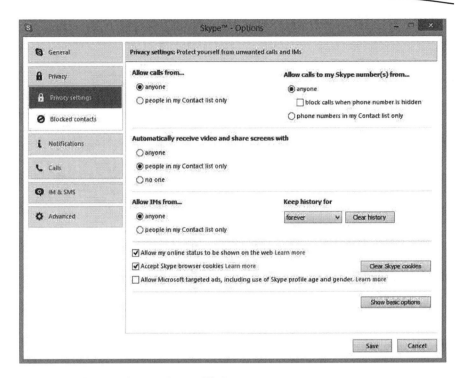

Figure 2-16. Skype's privacy settings on Windows

In Skype for Mac, similar settings are available at Skype | Preferences | Privacy (see Figure 2-17).

Figure 2-17. Skype for Mac privacy settings

For example, consider whether you want your picture to be visible to anyone who searches Skype's contact directory or only to your contacts. Do you want old friends and ex-colleagues to be able to identify you easily? How about potential business connections? People are usually more likely to reach out if they can put a face to the name and be sure they have the right person.

Security and Safety of Skype Communications

As for identity and safety, check out Skype's Online Safety page at `http://www.skype.com/intl/en-us/security/online-safety/` to ensure you are up-to-date with the latest issues that can affect both the security and privacy surrounding your use of Skype. Important points include:

- Keep your password to yourself and update it about twice a year.

- If on a Windows PC, install appropriate security software, such as available from Symantec, McAfee, Zone Alarm, Trend Micro, Panda, and other security software offerings.

- Always set Windows and Mac OSX to do regular operating system updates. Microsoft always releases a monthly update on the second Tuesday of the month; if there are urgent updates required, they will deliver them when necessary.

- Avoid downloading email attachments from unknown senders.

- Never respond to an email requesting your account login information (this applies to any service of which you are a member, such as eBay, Facebook, Twitter, YouTube, etc.); that's phishing.

- Only enter into your Skype profile information you are comfortable with making public. For instance, you may decide you are comfortable with entering your country, province/state, work and mobile phone numbers, but not your city or home phone number.

- Set Skype privacy settings you are comfortable with: Tools | Options | Privacy in Skype for Windows; Skype | Preferences | Privacy in Mac OSX.

- Block contacts who request access with no known reason; there is an option when blocking to "Report for Abuse." Skype monitors these reports and closes persistently abusive accounts.

From its initial launch, strong encryption technologies have been incorporated into Skype to prevent unauthorized access to your conversation content. As a result, other than a one-time blunder involving chat conversations in building a special Skype client only for use in China, there have been no reported cases of intrusion into Skype conversations.

There has been much controversy about Skype access by law enforcement agencies; however, Microsoft states that they will only provide access when required by law—which requires a warrant. At the time of writing the author has not seen any verified incidents of access over the nine years of following Skype. However, while Microsoft and other Internet publishers would like to disclose information about any access by government agencies, they are not permitted to do so by security law. And what they could provide would only be call detail records providing names of connected parties along with time and duration of calls (otherwise called metadata).

Calls to the legacy phone networks' landlines and mobile phones can be wiretapped once they pass outside to these networks; however, that is not an issue that Skype or Microsoft can control.

Keep in mind that tracking billions of minutes of calls would require a phenomenal amount of resources; as a result, unless you are involved in some potentially illicit activity Skype's inherent encryption addresses privacy issues with respect to your calling activity. But on the other hand, ensure you follow the guidelines mentioned earlier to maintain the integrity of your Skype account and your conversations.

Summary

Getting started with Skype involves installing the Skype software or app, creating a Skype account, incorporating your Skype Profile, and building a contacts directory.

Connecting to the Internet is also a basic requirement for using Skype. How you connect depends on whether your connection is made in a home office or while on the road.

This chapter covered the considerations for establishing a Skype account and maintaining not only the connection at a home office but also when making a connection at a remote road warrior location.

Key Points

- At a minimum a Skype account requires a unique Skype ID and an associated email address. But you can optionally add personal information such as time zone, location, birthday and legacy phone numbers.

- At a home office, connections can be made by either a wired Ethernet or Wi-Fi connection to an Internet modem/router.

- While on the road, wired connections may be available in some hotels; otherwise wireless connection over a Wi-Fi access point or a wireless carrier data plan is necessary.

- With Wi-Fi connections you need to understand why some connections may be robust enough for chat and voice calls but not for video calls.

- With carrier connections you need a multi-GB data plan subscription from your home carrier or, when roaming on a foreign carrier, a lower-cost alternative to simply making an *ad hoc* data connection to that carrier.

- Building a Skype Contacts (People) directory allows you to readily initiate conversations, whether as a Skype contact or a phone number.

- Only with Skype Contacts can a user take full advantage of all Skype's features.

- Status provides information on your availability for participating in a conversation.

- Favorites provide a way to easily access Contacts with whom a user has frequent conversations, especially on Skype for mobile devices.

- Skype allows you to customize your privacy options, so you can control who you receive calls and instant messages from, who can see your profile photo, and more. It is a good idea to review these settings when you first start using Skype.

- Skype voice and chat conversations are highly encrypted, but you must still take care with measures such as keeping your password secure and keeping your hardware and software up to date.

Chapter 3

Enriching Conversations with Skype

Having established a Skype account, built a Contact directory and made an Internet connection, it's time to take a look at how Skype can enrich conversations using its unique mix of features that support archiving, sharing, and collaboration—whether on a PC or a mobile device.

Enhancing and Moving Beyond the Voice Conversation

In the past, making a voice call over a telephone was simple. With legacy telephone calls you would simply dial a number and hope someone, whose status was unknown, would answer—if not, maybe it would go to voice mail. At the other end the phone would ring; the recipient, if present at the phone, could decide whether to answer or, if provisioned, let it go to voice mail. In any case, the recipient's activities when called would usually be interrupted; the incoming call took priority, regardless of who was calling or what the recipient was doing at the time. And once there was engagement it was only a voice conversation.

As users became familiar with Skype that random access process and in-conversation activity changed. From new etiquette for engagement to supporting the conversation using Skype's complementary features, a Skype conversation in a business setting not only overcomes the geographical barriers to a voice conversation or conference room meeting, but also transforms physical office activities into a virtual office setting:

- **Is anybody there?** Presence information tells you a contact's status, whether they are available or away, are offline, or not wanting to be disturbed.

- **Knock on the door, asking permission to enter:** With Skype it is considered good etiquette to use Skype chat to see whether the other party is available and only call at an agreed on time—whether immediately, in five minutes, or five hours.

- **Water fountain conversations:** Sustainable group chat sessions become virtual water fountain conversations in which participants make contributions and comments on an *ad hoc* basis and these conversations also can be archived and searched on a PC.

- **The virtual notebook:** During a voice or video conversation, the chat session remains available to make notes of ideas, comments, goals, follow up, and so on, related to the conversation. The bonus with Skype chat is that these notes become archived on a PC and searchable for later recall.

- **Leaving paperwork and photographs on a colleague's desk:** File transfer delivers documents, drawings, and even books to a chat participant. Or deliver these items through a cloud storage service URL, such as Dropbox or Microsoft OneDrive. In fact, in a single step, these can be delivered to multiple parties on a group chat.

- **Face-to-face encounters:** One consequence of Skype video is that participants can see others' facial expressions. When on the larger screen of a PC or even the iPad, it's almost like having the other party across the table. Skype's crystal clear audio and echo cancellation features make it sound like the other party is in the room with you.

- **Whiteboarding:** Chat becomes a medium for taking notes and sharing "spelling-specific" information, such as email addresses, contact information, and URLs. Screen sharing plays a significant role here also with its contribution to support or reinforce the conversation dialogue through virtual illustration of an issue.

- **Demonstrations:** Video allows a participant to support both internal and external conversations through screen sharing or a demonstration of a new physical product or, in a support scenario, show a customer how to physically fix, say, a hardware issue.

For road warriors Skype also complements their business use:

- Calling home from hotel rooms and other remote locations to enhance and support family relationships.

- Video calls in which parents can view their children's accomplishments of the day and assist them with, say, homework exercises.

- Family multi-party calls, bringing in relatives.

- Special interest group multi-party calls, such as golfing buddies, sports organizations/teams, and hobbies.

But that's only the start; what follows provides an overview on how a Skype-to-Skype conversation can evolve from an initial chat to a fully enriched business conversation.

Skype's Full Feature Set

The original and most comprehensive platform on which to experience Skype is Windows desktop. This experience is now matched by more recent versions of Skype on Mac OS X. On these platforms, Skype generates and supports conversations through:

- Voice calling (Skype-to-Skype, Skype-to/from landlines and mobile phones)

- Video calling (Skype-to-Skype)

- Hosting, and/or participating in, multi-party voice and video calls

- Presence or status

- Text messaging (chat, SMS)

- Group chat

- Conversation archiving (unlimited)
- Contact directory
- Multiple calling features including:
  - Voice mail
  - Video messaging
  - Call forwarding
  - File transfer
  - Screen sharing

You can access any of these features by selecting a Contact and using a menu associated with the Contact. See Figure 3-1 for what a right-click on a Contact in Skype for Windows Desktop shows.

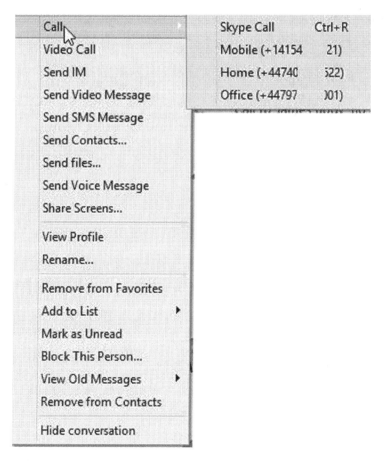

Figure 3-1. Skype's core features

> **Note**   Chapter 5 shows how to carry out these Skype functions on
> Windows desktop and Mac OS X. The functions available on mobile devices
> are generally more limited and these are covered in more detail in Chapter 6.

All the Skype features listed here are free, with the following exceptions:

- Calls to landlines and mobile phones (including
  participants on a multi-party call)

- SMS messaging

- Call forwarding to a landline or wireless number. Call
  forwarding to another Skype user is free.

More details and costs are discussed in Chapter 7.

SKYPE AND EMERGENCY CALLS

Skype is not a replacement for your mobile or fixed-line telephone. In particular, apart from
in very limited circumstances (Australia, Denmark, Finland, and UK), the software does
not allow you to make emergency calls to emergency services. You must make alternative
communication arrangements to ensure you can make emergency calls if necessary.

Conversation Flow

Conversations can easily escalate from chat to voice to video as the context
of the conversation evolves. It is now considered good etiquette to at least
ask, via a chat message, if the party is available to take a call.

Having agreed to at least chat it's helpful to follow how a typical
conversation sequence can evolve, in context, from chat to voice to video
(and optionally to screen sharing).

To start, select a contact from People/Contacts (using Contact search if
appropriate). In Figure 3-2 I'm searching for my contact Voice On The Web.

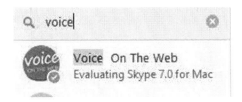

Figure 3-2. Finding a contact using search

To check whether a contact is available, start a chat conversation in the Conversation pane (for PC see Figure 3-3) or screen (mobile).

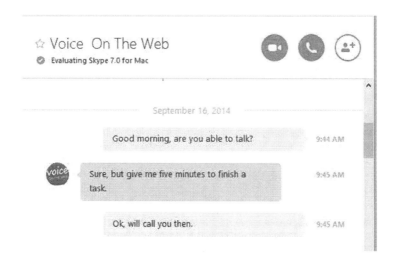

Figure 3-3. Using chat to see whether a contact is free

When ready, it's time to switch to a voice or video call. Figure 3-4 shows the options available for voice calling from a PC. The default is a call to a contact's Skype account.

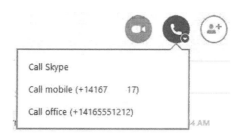

Figure 3-4. Voice calling options on a PC

Figure 3-5 shows the same options as they might appear on a mobile device.

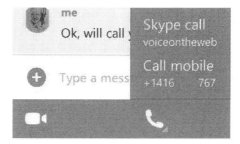

Figure 3-5. Voice calling options on a mobile device

If your call starts with voice only, you can choose to escalate to video at a later point using the video button (the left of four options in Figure 3-6), or you can tap or click on the + button to open the share menu seen in Figure 3-7.

Figure 3-6. A voice call in progress

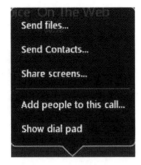

Figure 3-7. More options for enriching your conversation via the share menu

This gives you the option to share files or photos, add more people to the conversation, or share screens.

> **Note**   You can also use this menu to show the dial pad, which might be useful for example if you're calling into a conference bridge and need to enter a passcode.

The call management bar shown in Figure 3-6 and in more detail in Figure 3-8 is common to all Skype voice and video conversations. This is your route to the various options for enriching your Skype conversations.

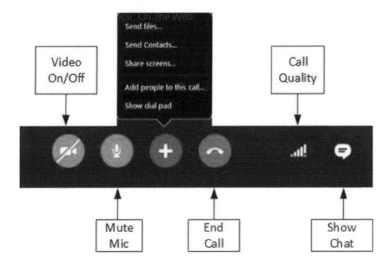

Figure 3-8. Call management bar (Skype 7 for Windows)

What is meant by enrichment? A conversation can be enriched using:

- File and/or photo/image transfer

- Screen sharing (from a participant on a PC)

- Add People for a multi-party call

- Chat to enter notes, URLs, email addresses, and other text-based information

- Share Skype contacts

With all its features, a Skype conversation can be very *ad hoc* in terms of what the next step is; at each stage there are several options for enhancing the conversation in context.

Skype's Unique Technology: Innovation for the Masses

As Skype evolved from free voice calling and instant messaging (presence and chat), it introduced new technologies that established the baseline for voice and video quality. Echo cancellation, crystal clear audio, and HD video are all now standard requirements for any Internet-based conversation service; however, Skype was the pioneer who introduced these qualities to the calling experience.

Emulating Face-to-Face Conversation Voice Quality

Since its launch in 2003, Skype has developed several technologies that establish its voice and video calling performance as benchmarks for overall audio and video quality.

Let's start by talking about the voice benchmarks in terms of benefits to the user.

- **Echo cancellation**[1] makes it possible to use the native microphone and speakers on a notebook (or suitably equipped desktop) without the echo that would otherwise occur when a call participant's microphone picks up and echoes the audio from the speakers.

---

[1]http://voiceontheweb.biz/2007/03/skype-32-sets-new-standard-for-sound-quality/

- **Skype's SILK technology**[2] ensures that Skype-to-Skype calls deliver crystal clear and distortion-free voice. The resulting "superwideband" audio quality is superior to what you hear on a call involving the conventional phone network, whether landline or mobile.

If you're using a modern stereo headset, it's SILK that makes remote parties on a call sound as if they are in-your-head. It significantly reduces the "could you repeat that" issues that can result from different accents or other distractive effects that could distort the remote party's speech.

Skype's SILK technology also self-adapts to underlying network conditions and provides optimum audio quality for connections to devices that support lower-quality (wideband or narrowband) audio.

> **Note**   As one unique application of Skype's SILK technology, musicians can give music lessons[3] or "private concerts"[4] online using Skype. Basically SILK captures and transmits all the harmonics of the musician's voice or instrument. This only applies for Skype-to-Skype calls.

Skype also has network connection monitoring routines that manage network issues in real time as network conditions change during a call to ensure your call connection is continuously optimized. The most recent version of Skype for Windows Desktop even attempts to automatically restore a connection if lost for some reason.

Beyond echo cancellation and SILK technology, one outstanding issue affecting the calling environment has been the background noise environment you're in when making or receiving a call—an airport, train station, shopping mall, or rock concert. However, taking advantage of phones with multiple microphones, such as more recent Microsoft Lumia phones and BlackBerry Passport, Skype has introduced audio processing technology. In these situations, signals from all the microphones are combined using the phone's inherent smart signal processing technology to zoom in to your voice and cancel everything else.

---

[2]http://voiceontheweb.biz/2009/02/silk-skypes-new-audio-codec-sets-new-performance-standards-for-voice-conversations/
[3]http://mukilteobeacon.villagesoup.com/news/story/skype-helps-local-musician-share-lessons-with-the-online-world/226100/
[4]http://mashable.com/2012/03/14/denison-witmer-skype-concerts/

Evolving to HD Video

Skype has also played a key role in the evolution of image quality in video calls. Today, the video image quality is excellent on both PCs and mobile devices, provided there is enough Internet bandwidth. There are two different levels of video:

- **Skype High Quality Video:** Skype pioneered High Quality Video with its launch in the fall of 2007,[5] including these three key features:

    - 640 x 480 (VGA) resolution at 30 frames per second

    - Kept the minimum user Internet connection upload speed to a level offered by most broadband Internet services (512 Kbps)

    - Takes advantage of Logitech webcams or the webcams incorporated into more recent PC and laptop display panels

- **Skype HD Video:** In late 2010 Skype introduced support for HD Video (720p),[6] including these three features:

    - 720p resolution at 22 frames per second (30 fps on Logitech webcams)

    - Kept the minimum user Internet connection upload speed to the 1.2 Mbps offered by most broadband Internet services as an option

    - Required a Skype-certified HD video webcam from Logitech or other vendors or the webcam on Macs offered in June 2011 or later.

When High Quality and HD video were first introduced, Skype certified certain vendors' webcams for optimum video call performance. However, by 2013 the hardware technology had evolved to the point where most third-party webcams and embedded webcams provided as standard on notebook PCs and PC displays support HD video, often at 1080p resolution.

---

[5]http://voiceontheweb.biz/tag/high-quality-video-launch/
[6]http://voiceontheweb.biz/2010/12/skype-for-windows-5-0-upgrade-the-return-of-hd-video-calling/

Smartphones and tablets introduced since 2013 also support HD video, with not only 720p but also 1080p resolutions. In 2014 Skype introduced upgrades to their mobile and tablet applications to support either HD video resolutions or "quarter-HD" video (960 x 540).

Rich Conversation in Action: Skype as a Support Tool

There are many scenarios in which Skype's features can add value to a conversation. One example I often encounter is Skype's usefulness as a support tool. I often receive queries about PC usage, involving not only Skype but also other applications. When feasible I suggest using Skype to help resolve the other party's issue. For example, you can:

- ▓ Use chat to discuss an issue, either in real time, or as and when you have time available. Chat has become my primary conversation mode; when it comes to support it remains so, especially given that messages can be left to be picked up when the other user comes online or accesses his Skype account from any device. Chat is ideal during a voice or video call to record notes and exchange links that complement the conversation.

- ▓ Use screen sharing to have the user demonstrate the issue she is encountering. Screen sharing opens up a real-time window into the other user's desktop to either see what they are doing or to provide monitored guidance complementing the conversation.

- ▓ Use SnagIt screen captures with file transfer to demonstrate how an item should appear or to have the other user highlight a particular point. Screen capture to image transfer only requires four clicks: Share | Send to Skype | Select Contact | Send. This works only for transfer to a single contact; sending to a Group Chat requires the more cumbersome process of saving a screen capture and then using file transfer to send the saved file.

- ▓ Enter a URL in the chat window to provide instant access to a resource that may address the issue. Click the link to browse a website supporting the conversation or to send an email that complements the conversation.

While most support calls require only a voice connection, there are times—in context of the discussion—when a video call can expedite resolution. Facial expressions contribute to comprehension; of course video can also be used to demonstrate hardware or how to fix an item.

Support activity is best suited to Skype on a Mac or a PC with its complete feature set (including screen sharing).

Summary

Skype is more than simply making voice calls; it takes everyday physical office activities and transforms them into a virtual office that allows a business to overcome geographical barriers and build businesses worldwide without all the travel expense. Three use cases outlining how Skype has contributed to a business's growth are covered in Chapter 4.

While users can make voice calls to legacy landline and mobile phone numbers, establishing Skype Contact relationships is critical to taking advantage of Skype's many conversation enrichment features.

Having covered Skype's full feature set and conversation flow, it's time to move on to talking about how these features are used in practice to create rich Skype conversations within both business and personal communications activities.

Key Points

Skype's features allow business teams to enrich conversations through sharing desktops, exchanging documents and graphics through file transfer, adding contacts to create multi-party calls, as well as logging and archiving all conversation activity for later recall.

Skype also supports personal relationships on the road through family calls, video calls, or catching up with special interest groups.

A Skype call can start as a simple voice call, and then seamlessly evolve in to video. It's also easy to add people to a conversation on the fly, share screens, and send files or photos during the call.

Skype's audio and video technologies deliver crystal clear voice and high-quality HD video across all platforms. Amongst other benefits, crystal clear voice reduces "can you repeat that" requests and permits music education over Skype.

Chapter 4

Using Skype in Business—Use Cases

According to statistics issued in the past 35%–40% of Skype activity involves business use. As mentioned earlier Skype has helped many startups and small businesses grow their operations worldwide and take geography out of the barriers to growth. Businesses can hire the best personnel from a worldwide pool of talent; they can find the best suppliers for a project or building hardware and, most importantly, they can market their offerings worldwide.

For this book, three companies have offered to tell their story about how they use Skype and how it makes their operations more productive and more profitable, especially through reduced communications and overhead costs (such as travel).

zenPeak—Recruiting Executives with a Social Algorithm

zenPeak is a combination of an executive search firm, alongside a tech development arm deploying location-based technology on mobile smartphones. Operating out of Toronto, Canada zenPeak has a local staff of home-based recruiters filling positions at businesses in southern Ontario managed by CEO Frank Abrams. The HR services are complemented by a smartphone application built by developers in India, created for resale to HR departments. With a customer base primarily in southern Ontario and employees working from home offices, Skype has become a valuable tool for ongoing virtual water fountain conversations using Skype Group Chat.

On the other hand Frank manages a team of developers in India who are several time zones away. Aside from using chat, there are frequent one-to-one voice calls and occasional group voice or video calls, especially when launching a new project.

Frank reflected on their use of Skype with the following comments:

- Skype is platform agnostic and empowers employees to decide on their PC and/or mobile devices.

    - Employees and developers can follow and participate in conversations whether on PCs or mobile devices.

    - When they leave their home office, conversations continue to flow on their mobile device.

- It's available 24/7; comments can be made at any time in various chat sessions. Frank receives calls from India at any time, often when it's overnight at the home base. From India he frequently gets calls simply to clarify an issue.

- When launching a new product development phase, Frank often needs 60 to 90 minutes to explain the goals and details of the work via a group voice call to the developer team in India. Basically, Skype becomes a virtual conference room for these presentations.

- The developers often use screen sharing to reinforce a discussion.

- They make frequent use of file transfer to send a screen capture related to the product under development (using MW Snap but could also use SnagIt).

To quote Frank:

Skype has become critical to zenPeak's operations, not simply because most services are free but because it goes beyond voice connections. Skype's enriched communications features facilitate zenPeak's business processes and make our operations more productive.

Bicymple—Innovative Bicycle Re-Engineering

Bicymple LLC. is a small business located in Bellingham, WA, USA that sells the innovative and unique bicycle, "the bicymple." The bicymple is stylish, fun, and unlike any other bike on the market thanks to its direct-drive system and symmetrical front and rear steering. The bicymple was brought to market via crowdfunding and the company makes extensive use of the available digital tools to get business done.

Josh Bechtel and Gabe Starbuck have created a successful manufacturing startup out of thin air, built around an innovative redesign of one of the world's most ubiquitous pieces of equipment. More details on their unique design can be found on the Bicymple website (`http://www.bicymple.com/`).

Skype facilitates building relationships with suppliers, distributors, designers, and fabricators—both across town and across the planet. Deploying Skype on Windows, Mac, and Android phones and tablets they benefit from:

- Skype-to-Skype voice and video calls, including Group calls

- Group chats

- Individual chat

- Screen sharing

Skype provides the underlying communications platform for virtual water fountain conversations, customer sales activities, document sharing, demonstrations, PowerPoint presentations, team meetings, and individual one-to-one chat conversations.

Skype helps with:

- Sourcing parts from other experts in Washington State, California, and The United Kingdom while collaborating with a 150-year-old unicycle hub manufacturer in Switzerland.

- Getting in touch with an audience of bike enthusiasts and consumers around the world. Proud new owners of Bicymples can be found from Germany to The United Arab Emirates to Australia.

- Reducing travel and startup costs associated with building up production facilities.

To quote Josh:

> *It's really cool to use Skype[1] to connect with other designers to make sure the product is exactly what we need it to be. We can see changes real-time, kind of looking over their shoulder digitally and see what they're working on.*

The bottom line is that by employing Skype's many features beyond the voice call, Skype has contributed to their "lean startup" approach to manufacturing.

Advansys—Software Solutions Building Business Productivity

Advansys, established in 1989, is an Australian software development company specializing in innovative business solutions. Advansys' solutions have included council document automation, mobile device synchronization software, email client extension and developer tools, user and administrator managed archiving, and data conversion solutions.

Advansys is a mature, dynamic organization with the partnerships and commercial and technical experience to assist organizations to maximize their collaboration investment. Advansys has been using Skype since 2004.

Quoting Advansys Managing Director Greg Bell from an updated version of a post originally appearing in the Skype Big Blog:[2]

"When Skype came along it was a fantastic opportunity for our small business to cut costs," Bell says. International calls from Australia came with a high price tag, and Bell's staff often spoke with customers at length.

Fast forward 12 years, and Bell relies on Skype Manager[3], Instant Messaging, Calling Plan subscriptions, online numbers[4], and call forwarding[5] to maintain

---

[1]http://www.skype.com/en/?intcmp=blogs-_-generic-click-_-bicycle-startup-gears-up-with-group-video-calling
[2]http://blogs.skype.com/2012/08/02/advansys-employees-find-work-1/
[3]http://www.skype.com/intl/en-us/business/skype-manager/?intcmp=blogs-_-generic-click-_-advansys-employees-find-work-1
[4]http://www.skype.com/intl/en-us/features/allfeatures/online-number/?intcmp=blogs-_-generic-click-_-advansys-employees-find-work-1
[5]http://www.skype.com/intl/en-us/features/allfeatures/call-forwarding/?intcmp=blogs-_-generic-click-_-advansys-employees-find-work-1

constant communication with employees, partners, and customers. Video calling[6] and screen sharing[7] enhance dealings with external partners. He and his staff also are devotees of ongoing group chats.

> **Tip** To make it easier to find valuable information within Skype chat conversations later, Advansys employees use hashtags such as #todo or #idea in ongoing chats.

"Skype is the central nervous system of our business," says Bell. "We're fully virtualized—all our staffers work from home."

Years ago, Bell experienced the frustrations of downtime and traffic when he traveled the area as a computer engineer for HP. His four core staff members are spread throughout the suburbs of Sydney, a city of more than 4.6 million people. When Advansys went virtual, one employee gained back nearly 20 hours each week.

"They appreciate having the extra time to spend with their families or to do whatever they enjoy," Bell says. *"It's a major improvement in quality of life. It's not only time and productivity—I think you live longer if you can avoid the traffic!"*

But Skype's not all business for Bell. At one point he traveled frequently abroad, meaning less time to spend with his wife and three children. He recalls sitting in the waiting lounge of the airport in Frankfurt, Germany, taking advantage of Skype and free Wi-Fi[8] to talk to his small son while playing a building simulation game together online.

"It was amazing. I could hear him clearly and be playing with him in a virtual environment," says Bell. *"It made us feel so close to each other and yet we were half a world apart."*

At one point, Bell's teenage daughter fell ill and ended up in the hospital. Bell stayed close by as she recovered, using Skype from the waiting room to keep his business running.

---

[6]http://www.skype.com/intl/en-us/features/allfeatures/video-call/?intcmp=blogs-_-generic-click-_-advansys-employees-find-work-l
[7]http://www.skype.com/intl/en-us/features/allfeatures/screen-sharing/?intcmp=blogs-_-generic-click-_-advansys-employees-find-work-l
[8]http://www.skype.com/intl/en/features/allfeatures/skype-wifi/?intcmp=blogs-_-generic-click-_-advansys-employees-find-work-l

"Being online and being available is essential, particularly in our fast-moving business," Bell says.

What's next for Advansys? Not only does the company count on Skype for business collaboration and family ties, it has built a product to be used in conjunction with Skype. RecollX, the company's first Skype-related product, allows users to archive their full written chat history, search it with what Bell calls an "industrial strength search engine," and then export to the application of their choice.

And today Advansys continues to use Skype.

Their employees communicate with their customers and sales partners using Skype on Windows PCs, iPhones, iPad, Android phones, and Windows 8 Phones (see Chapters 5 and 6 for details of how to use Skype on these platforms).

They use all the features of Skype, including group chat, voice, and video to support:

- Virtual water fountain conversations (via Group chat)

- Customer sales activities

- Customer service support

- Customer tech support

- Screen sharing for document sharing, demonstrations and PowerPoint presentations

- File/photo sharing (or screen capture sharing via SnagIt)

- Team meetings

- Individual one-to-one chat

- Team or staff training

Advansys Managing Director Greg Bell stated that:

We use Skype chat very heavily for documenting discussions, decisions during meetings, and documenting core elements of our product development process. As a result, Skype history is a critical resource and we, through necessity, developed RecollX to handle archiving and research of large volumes of Skype history.

Summary

These three businesses are representative of how Skype has become a critical tool not only for low cost communications but also building business relationships worldwide. Leveraging a small employee base they are able to maintain sustainable contact across time zones and create a productive business environment.

Enrichment of Skype conversations using file transfer and screen sharing has been discussed in Chapter 3. The remainder of this book provides guidance on how to use the various Skype features mentioned in this chapter:

- Details on using Skype on PCs and mobile devices are covered in Chapters 5 and 6.

- Chat, the most used feature of Skype, is covered in Chapter 8.

- How business teams can build synergy and success with Skype's collaboration features such as screen sharing, group calling, and group chat are discussed in Chapter 11.

- Using Skype with landlines and mobile phones is discussed in Chapter 7. This is complemented by the associated discussion on payments, subscriptions, and managing your Skype account in Chapter 9.

Chapter 5

Using Skype on the Desktop

So far the discussion has covered how Skype can contribute to more effective business processes, how to set up an account, and how to build a Skype Contact directory. Now let's turn to using Skype on its many supported PC, smartphone, and tablet platforms.

Skype is fundamentally a software application that supports various modes of conversation. Since its launch as a Windows application in late August 2003 versions have become available for Mac OS X and Linux PCs; new features ranging from calling landlines and mobile phones to video calling have been introduced over its first decade. This chapter covers using Skype on Windows PCs and Macs.

In April 2009 Skype introduced its first application for mobile smartphones–Skype for iPhone–with a very limited feature set. Today Skype is available on all iOS (iPhone, iPad, iPod Touch), Android, BlackBerry 10, Windows Phone 8, and Amazon Fire devices with an almost complete feature set, including support for HD video resolutions. Using Skype on mobile devices is covered in Chapter 6.

With Microsoft's acquisition of Skype in late 2011, Skype access has become integrated into Outlook 2010 and 2013, and Outlook.com (Microsoft's web mail replacement for Hotmail). In addition, Skype has been hooked up with Microsoft Lync, Microsoft's enterprise communications application. In early 2015, Microsoft will also make Skype available for making and receiving calls within a web browser and introduce Skype for

Office Online, which provides Skype chat while collaborating on a Word or PowerPoint document. More details on these integrations are provided in Chapter 12.

Consistent with Microsoft's policy of providing automatic updates for Windows and Office, Skype updates are now automatic on all platforms; this is becoming more important for both maintaining compatibility across devices as Skype's backend infrastructure is modified and upgraded and addressing any security issues.

Once you have a Skype account, have established a few contacts, and have an Internet connection in place, you can start making (and receiving) calls using your Skype client or application. The basic process for placing a call is

- Select a Contact

- Find the Phone or Webcam icon and click on the icon to launch a voice or video call, respectively

- Within the context of the call, share files, add participants, and exchange text-based information in the Chat pane.

The details differ by platform; in this chapter we'll cover the details behind making a call on Windows and Mac OS X desktops.

THE FACEBOOK CONNECTION

For the past few years, Skype has included an option to Connect to Facebook on both the Windows and Mac client's home page. This connection provides:

- Incorporation of your Facebook news feed summaries into the home page display.

- Addition of your Facebook Contacts into your Contacts directory, including any landline or mobile phone numbers in their Facebook profiles. Contacts can optionally be displayed using the Contacts drop-down menu.

Features relating to the Facebook connection and Facebook Contacts appear throughout this chapter.

Skype for Windows Desktop

Skype for Windows was the original Skype software launched in August 2003. It has been continuously updated over the years to incorporate calling to landlines and mobile phones (originally called SkypeOut), SMS messaging, echo cancellation[1], the SILK codec[2] for crystal-clear audio quality on Skype-to-Skype calls, High Quality (VGA) Video[3], HD Video[4], optional Facebook integration[5] and, most recently, video messaging.

Skype for Windows continues to be the most feature-rich version and can be used to manage all your Skype calling activity in terms of managing Contacts, hosting multi-party calls, building groups, sharing files, checking your audio and video hardware, and archiving your Skype conversation activity. It's all done using the Skype for Windows Desktop client shown in Figure 5-1.

---

[1]http://voiceontheweb.biz/2007/03/skype-32-sets-new-standard-for-sound-quality/
[2]http://voiceontheweb.biz/2009/02/silk-skypes-new-audio-codec-sets-new-performance-standards-for-voice-conversations/
[3]http://voiceontheweb.biz/tag/high-quality-video-launch/
[4]http://voiceontheweb.biz/2010/12/skype-for-windows-5-0-upgrade-the-return-of-hd-video-calling/
[5]http://voiceontheweb.biz/2011/06/skype-for-windows-5-5-beta-first-impressions-with-facebook-integration/

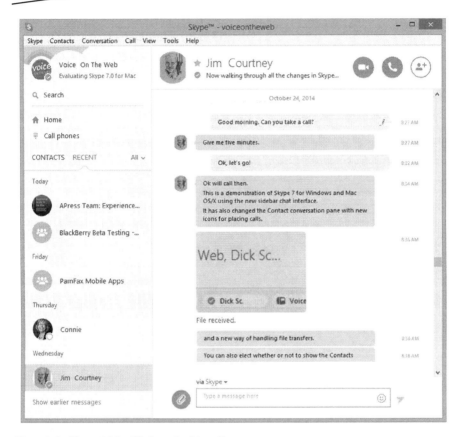

Figure 5-1. Skype 7.0 for Windows Desktop client

As mentioned earlier, Skype upgrades Skype for Windows every two or three months. While often introducing new features, they may also include modifications of existing features–with the intention of improving the user experience. Concurrently Skype is upgrading the "back office" infrastructure to both add more features and make the calling experience more reliable and robust. While there are manual upgrade methods available via the Skype Garage blog, once an upgrade version is shown to be stable for a few days, Skype automatically offers to upgrade your installation.

The discussion in this section reflects the user interface when using Skype 7 for Windows Desktop, which introduced several incremental changes[6] that modified and enhanced the user experience.

---

[6]http://voiceontheweb.biz/skype-world/skype-software/skype-5-10-windows-revised-contacts-management/

> **Tip**   Follow Voice On The Web[7] for information on changes as new versions come out.

The Skype for Windows client has three main elements:

- A Personal pane that provides access to your Skype Profile (click on your own name at the top), as well as an icon menu with access to a Skype Home Page incorporating your Facebook News feed and/or contacts' Skype mood messages, a dial pad (Call Phones), group creation, and new contacts search.

- A Contacts pane on the left side, below the Personal pane, where you can build your Contacts directory and launch your calling activity via the Contacts tab and the Recent activity tab showing the Contacts or Groups with whom you have communicated recently.

- A Conversation pane on the right side that contains not only your chat messages with a selected Contact (or Group) but also a log of all your other Skype activity with the selected Contact such as calls made and files transferred. Internet URLs, including website and email addresses, are automatically converted into actionable links.

The Conversation pane content is archived on your local PC and is searchable (Ctrl-F) to recover information going back to when chat communication with the Contact commenced. It is most useful for recovering URLs exchanged, discussion records, and other chat information. A more detailed discussion of using the Conversation pane is covered in Chapter 8.

---

[7]http://voiceontheweb.biz/tag/skype-for-windows/

> **Note**   There are two ways to use Skype on Windows 8 and 8.1: by using
> Skype for Windows Desktop as discussed in this chapter, or by using the
> Windows 8 Skype app. The second option is covered in Chapter 6 because
> it follows the same user experience as Skype on mobile devices. This option
> is available on any device with any version of Windows 8 or 8.1 installed,
> including Microsoft's Surface and other vendors' Windows 8 tablets, whereas
> desktop Skype is only available on devices with a full version of Windows 8 or
> 8.1, such as Surface Pro models and any desktop or laptop PC.

The Personal Pane

The Personal pane, shown in Figure 5-2, provides access to your Skype
Profile (click on your name at the top) as well as a Skype Home page, a dial
pad, and contact search.

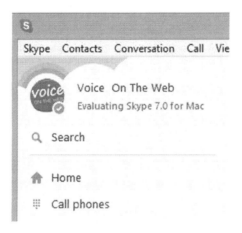

Figure 5-2. Skype for Windows Desktop Personal pane

The Skype home page (see Figure 5-3) summarizes recent activity in the
form of a text box for changing your Skype Mood Message and content
selected from any of your Facebook News Feed (if you have elected to log
into Facebook), your Skype Contacts' Mood Messages, Alerts Messages
from Skype, or all three. It's really a personal choice as to which you follow
and can easily be changed.

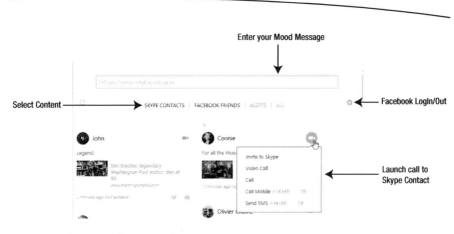

Figure 5-3. *Skype for Windows Desktop home page*

Mousing over the webcam image beside a Facebook Friend's name opens a menu to call them on Skype or call them at their home, mobile, or work phone via calling to landline or mobile numbers in their Facebook profile.

Selecting Call Phones opens up a dial pad, see Figure 5-4, in the Conversation pane. Depending on the width of your Skype client (simply widen or narrow the Skype window) you will see:

Figure 5-4. *Skype for Windows Desktop dial pad*

You can either enter a phone number directly or start to enter a Contact's name and a dialog frame opens in which phone number options appear, if phone numbers have been entered into a Contact's profile.

The Contacts Pane

Think of the Contacts pane (see Figure 5-5) as a combination of your personal phonebook, call-by-name "dialer" and archived conversation selector. Select a Contact from the Contacts or Recent tabs and, in the Conversation pane, you can:

- Enter a text message to that Contact

- Launch a voice or video call with the Contact

- Send an SMS message, if the Contact has identified a mobile phone number in his/her Skype Profile

- Send files, photos, or a video message

- Send a Skype Contact profile

- View previous messages and conversation history

- Search the Contact's conversation history for past messages, call detail records, web URLs, and file transfers.

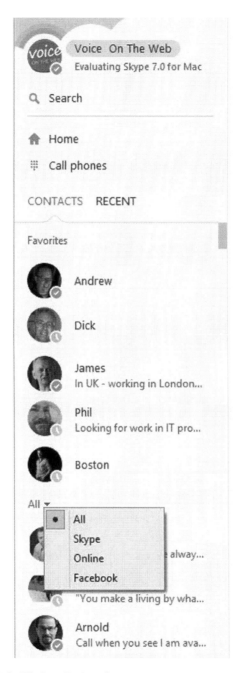

Figure 5-5. Skype 7.0 for Windows Desktop Contact pane

When using the Contact pane there are several other tips that can help your overall use of Skype:

- Contacts have the option to enter their Work/Mobile/ Home phone numbers; they are available via View Profile in a Contact's right-click menu. When they do not enter them into their public profile you can now enter them into a Contact's information on your local PC (see Figure 5-6):

  a. Select a Contact.

  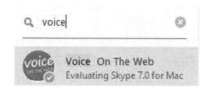

  b. Right-click and select View Profile.

  c. Select Add Number.

  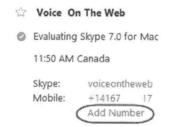

d.   Select Mobile, Home, Office, or Other.

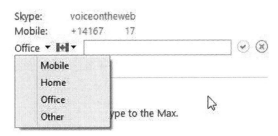

e.   Select a country.

f.   Enter the contact's phone number.

g. Click the check mark on the right to complete entry
    of the phone number into the Profile seen on the
    local PC; (note also that it is editable).

Skype: voiceontheweb
Mobile: +14167   17
Office: +14165551212   Edit
          Add Number

h. Either click the number in the Profile or the Call icon
    in the Conversation pane header to initiate a call to
    the number.

■   You can rename a Contact to make it more readily
    identifiable. Right-click the Contact's name in the
    Contacts or Recent tab, and select Rename. This is
    useful when a Contact fails to enter their full name or
    only has a SkypeID showing. (How many of your friends
    are named John or Mary?) Note that Rename only
    appears on your local PC. You must make this change
    on each device where your account is logged in.

■   To search for a Contact, enter a name in the Contacts
    Search bar and the Contact tab will filter down the
    Contacts list to those names containing the text you
    have entered.

With Skype 7 for Windows there is also an option to show Contact names in either a Contact Sidebar View with no profile images (View | Contact Sidebar View) or a default view that includes profile images. A List (or Category) is simply a subset of your Contacts in Skype for Windows; here are some details.

- There is some confusion between Lists and Groups. A List is an identified subset of all your Contacts. You may identify them as Work colleagues, a special interest group name, or any other subset that you feel appropriate. A Group is a set of your Contacts participating in a Group conversation.

- To set up a List, in the main Skype menu , go to Contacts | Contact Lists | Create a New List (see Figure 5-7) or, alternatively, right-click any Contact name and select Add to List, then select Create New List.

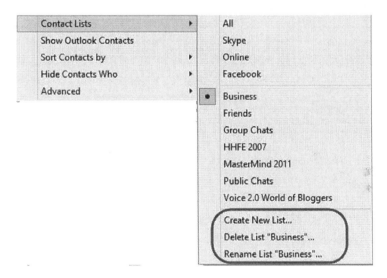

Figure 5-7. Contact Lists

- Add Contacts to a List simply using Add to List on the right-click menu for any Contact and selecting the desired List.

To filter your displayed Contacts by Lists there are two options:

- Go to the drop-down menu immediately below your Favorites and select a List; note there are four priority Categories: All, Skype, Online, and Facebook.

- From the main Skype menu select Contacts | Contact Lists and a similar menu appears. Note that towards the end of this menu there is also an option to create a List.

In Skype for Windows as mentioned elsewhere, a Group is created solely for the establishment of a multi-party Group conversation, whether Chat, Voice, or Video. Groups are created via the Create a Group icon in the Personal pane and are maintained in your Contacts tab for later recall. Groups also show up in the Recent tab if they have been recently active. If you add People during a call (via the + menu in the Call Management bar), a Group is created that appears under the Recent tab after ending the call.

If you have logged into Facebook, your Facebook friends will appear on the Facebook List or in All.

The Conversation Pane

The Conversation Pane, on the right side of the Skype window, builds a persistent archive of all your Skype activity with each individual Contact and Group. On selection of a Contact in the Contacts pane the Conversation pane:

- Stores and recalls conversation history by Contact or Group going back in time to the "Beginning" (when you first exchanged a message with the Contact or Group).

- Includes a pane at the bottom for text entry (along with emoticons).

- Allows you to share a file/photo, send a video message, or exchange a Contact profile by clicking the paperclip icon to the left of the text pane.

- Records voice and video call details: time of call, duration of call (also known as a call detail record or CDR).

- Records file sharing activity with an active link to both the file and the folder in which it was stored.

- Converts any website URLs and email addresses entered to active links.

- Permits editing or removal of a message for up to an hour after it has been posted.

Messages and other information are recorded with the most recent item at the bottom of the window. Note there is a time associated with each entry; if you scroll up you will also find date dividers. More details on Chat and its archiving activities are covered in Chapter 8.

> **Tip** A Skype account can be open on multiple PCs and mobile devices concurrently. Skype's infrastructure supports bringing up message history for an account when logging in to Skype on a different device.
>
> If you want to ensure that you always have a long-term, searchable history of your Skype conversations, always leave Skype for Windows or Skype for Mac open while traveling away from the home office and using Skype on a mobile device.

The Conversation pane can be optionally split off as a separate window using the View | Split Window View menu selection (see Figure 5-8). This way you can have a separate window for each Contact's chat session or each Group Chat activity.

Figure 5-8. Compact view–individual chat windows for each Contact or Group

When you are in this mode, double-click a Contact's name in the Contact pane (now a separate window) and a new window opens up with that Contact's conversation log. It is probably best to do this when you have a second display on which you can display only those chat sessions.

Return to the single window view via View | Default View.

For further discussion of Skype Chat, the conversation pane, and archiving your Skype conversation activity see Chapter 8.

Facebook Chat

If you have connected a Skype client with your Facebook account, a completely independent set of Contacts will show up in your Contacts pane, accessed through the Facebook tab. If you select to have a Facebook chat session, the Contact's name at the top of the conversation pane will have "Facebook" below the name (see Figure 5-9). Facebook messages are mirrored in Facebook Messenger apps on smartphones and tablets and on your Facebook page in a browser.

Figure 5-9. Facebook contact differentiation

The Conversation Pane Header

A significant feature of the Conversation pane is the set of Call icons in the Conversation Pane header for an individual Contact (see Figure 5-10).

Figure 5-10. Conversation pane header

To launch a call, select Video Call (camera icon) or Call (phone icon) as shown in Figure 5-10; with the latter you may also have to select how you want to call the Contact: Skype, Mobile, Office, Home.

The Add people icon brings up a list of all your Contacts from which you can select one or more to create a multi-party conversation session (see Figure 5-11). When you do this, the Call button changes to a Call Group button.

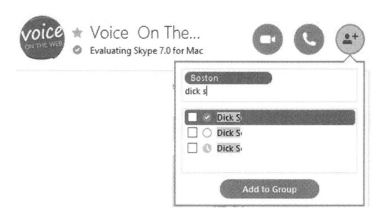

Figure 5-11. Add People, building a Group

Using the Webcam icon you can also launch a Group Video call
(see Figure 5-12).

Figure 5-12. Call Group

To the left of the text entry box at the bottom of the Conversation pane
is a paperclip icon. This launches a menu that gives you options to send
a photo/image, send a file (see the section "File Transfer"), send a video
message or send a contact. The last option sends the entire Skype profile
of any Contact that you choose to the selected Contact (see Figure 5-13).
Clicking the icon on the right brings up the emoticon selection panel.

Figure 5-13. Text entry box (with emoticons) and sharing options

File Transfer

There are five different ways to trigger a file transfer using Skype's File Transfer feature.

- **Method 1:** Right-click a Contact in the Contacts pane (either in the Contacts or Recent tab), and select Send files ....

- **Method 2:** Select the paperclip icon to the left of the text entry box, click Send File, and browse to the file you want to send. Note that when in a Group Chat or Call, the file can only be transferred to those members of the Group whom you have accepted as a Skype Contact.

■ **Method 3:** During a call, click the "+" symbol in the Call Management bar and select Send File…. When a file transfer occurs during a call, the transfer speed may be somewhat slower.

■ **Method 4:** In File Explorer, right-click any File name, select Send To, and select Skype in the drop-down menu.

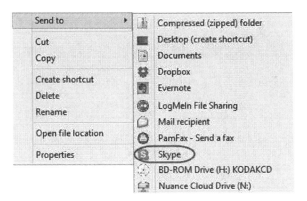

■ **Method 5:** Using the screen capture program SnagIt[8] you can add the Skype plugin that allows you to send a capture image directly to a Skype Contact as a file transfer. This is the file transfer method I use most frequently. It is very handy for complementing the conversation with live, in-context bug reporting or training and help.

[8]http://www.techsmith.com/snagit/

In October 2014, Skype started storing transferred files on the cloud such that file transfers remain available for recall by either the sender or receiver. If the cloud mode is fully supported in a Skype client or application you will see a thumbnail representing the file. In the case of an image, the thumbnail is of the image itself; for documents the thumbnail is an icon image of the application that is associated with the document's extension. Simply click the thumbnail to view the image in an application associated with the file extension. See Figure 5-14 for Skype 7 for Windows and Mac.

File Sent   File Received

Figure 5-14. File transfer Conversation pane images–sent and received

If a client has yet to support the cloud-based storage, there will be a URL to click to view the image (see Figure 5-15). This is a temporary situation until all clients support cloud-based file storage.

Figure 5-15. Interim file transfer records in Conversation pane

During a file transfer any active security software, such as Norton 360, will check for viruses.

A Skype Voice Call

On launching or accepting a Skype voice call, the Conversation pane becomes a dark background Call Screen (see Figure 5-16) and shows the profile image(s) of the called Contact(s) along with the Call Management bar, which includes icons for Show/Hide Chat, Show/Hide Contacts, and going to full screen display:

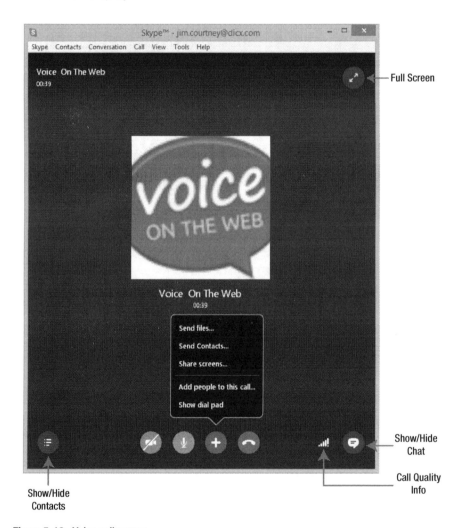

Figure 5-16. Voice call screen

Essential to managing the call is the Call Management bar at the bottom of the Call Screen. If it has disappeared after showing for several seconds, run your mouse over the lower portion of the Call Screen to bring it back.

Click the relevant icon to switch the webcam on/off, mute/unmute mic, end a call, access Call Quality Information, show/hide the Chat pane or, in the case of the "+" icon, to display a menu showing the sharing options. Call duration appears under the Skype profile picture of the calling party.

From within the Call Management Bar you can turn on/off full screen display (see Figure 5-16). However, there is also a call monitor window that is displayed whenever the user goes to another application on the desktop during a call. Running the cursor over this window brings up the mute/unmute and end call controls shown in Figure 5-17.

Figure 5-17. Call Monitor window

> **Tip**   Where is that Chat area?[9] When launching a call the Call screen
> takes up the entire Conversation pane (or Skype client if you hide
> Contacts). Click the Chat icon on the right side of the Call Management bar
> and, as shown in Figures 5-18 and 5-19, an area will appear at the bottom
> of, or on the right side of, the client window for chat messages that can
> complement and support the conversation.

[9]http://voiceontheweb.biz/2011/06/skype-5-x-chat-show-the-chat-window/

Becoming familiar with the use of the Call Management bar is fundamental to taking full advantage of Skype's call support features during a call.

During the call you can have a two- or three-panel screen comprising the Call Screen, Contacts, and/or Chat (see Figures 5-18 and 5-19).

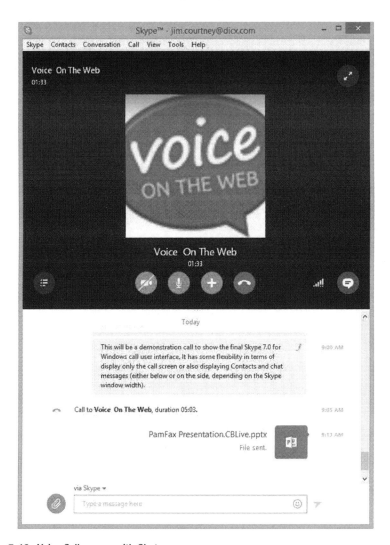

Figure 5-18. Voice Call screen with Chat–narrow

By widening the Skype client window the chat moves to a right sidebar (see Figure 5-19).

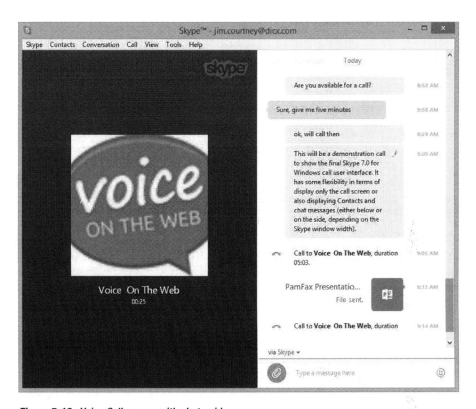

Figure 5-19. Voice Call screen with chat–wide

Click Show/Hide Contacts and you have the three panel client as shown in Figure 5-20.

Figure 5-20. Three panel screen: Contacts, Call, and Chat

If you have made a Skype-to-Skype call, you should have a crystal-clear voice connection. If not, use the Call Quality Info tool to determine whether your speakers, mic, webcam, and Internet connection are working properly.

Call Quality Info

The Call Quality Info feature (see Figure 5-21) allows you to easily check your audio/video hardware and Internet connection quality *in situ* during a call. This is a most useful and user friendly feature; when your mic/speaker doesn't work, the webcam video is fuzzy, and the Internet connection becomes weak. It provides a much simplified path for checking out any hardware issues during a call as opposed to checking via the Windows Control Panel or even Skype's Tools | Options utility–not exactly user friendly processes.

- Select a microphone and speak into it. While Automatic usually suffices, the option to manually adjust is there. Also there is the option to change the microphone being used in the call.

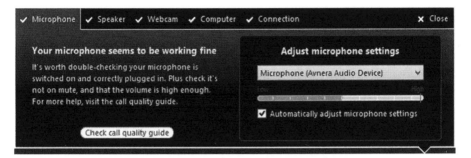

- The speaker tab allows you to change the speaker selection if you're not hearing the other party.

- You can select your webcam and check its image quality.

■ During a call you may also see the video status. Having a powerful enough PC does help with the overall call quality. At a minimum a multi-core processor, such as Intel's iCore series, is required for good video.

■ Finally, check the Connection status between the call participants.

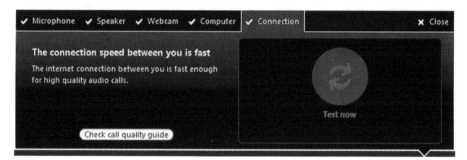

Should you lose your Internet connection Skype attempts to restore the connection for up to 60 seconds; if not restored it will end the call (see Figure 5-22).

Figure 5-22. Call connection recovery

When you complete a call (use the red End Call button on the Call Management bar or in a Call Monitor window), a Call Detail Record Entry (see Figure 5-23) is made in the Contact's Conversation pane showing who was called, the call duration, and when the call was terminated.

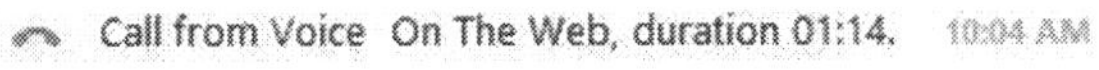

Call from Voice On The Web, duration 01:14.   10:04 AM

Figure 5-23. Call detail record

MAKING A SKYPE TEST CALL

If you want to test your mic, speakers, and webcam prior to making a call, place a call to Skype Test Call. This contact appears in your Contact list by default when you install Skype. It may also be called Echo / Sound Test Service or Skype Test Call (echo123). "Gertrude" explains how Skype Test Call works, gives you 10 seconds to say something, and then plays back what you said.

Next let's turn to making a video call.

A Skype Video Call

Provided your PC has a webcam, which can be checked out via the Call Quality Info icon in the Call Bar (or Tools | Options | General | Video Settings), a Skype video call is launched via the Video Call button (see Figure 5-24). However, a voice call can also be escalated to a video call using the Manage Video icon in the Call Management bar.

Figure 5-24. Video call screen

The Skype Video Call Management bar closely approximates the operation of a Skype voice call. A full screen display option (via the double arrow in the upper right of the Call pane) is incorporated as well as a Call Monitor window.

Of course, the other major difference is that the call screen also shows the video image in lieu of the Caller's Skype photo/avatar.

In this example both parties used webcams that supported HD video as you can tell by the wider (16:9) video window aspect ratio. Otherwise the video image will appear with the standard 4:3 aspect ratio.

The Video Call Monitor window (see Figure 5-25) pops up as a smaller window that remains available on the desktop whenever you go to another Windows application during the call. Note that controls can still be accessed for muting the mic and hanging up the call. While this window remains "always on top," it can be readily moved to any location on the desktop.

Figure 5-25. Video Call Monitor window

Finally, it is possible to show the video image full screen on the display monitor; in this case, for displays greater than 20 inches, one starts to approach a telepresence scenario.

Let's turn to one of the key sharing features available during a voice or video call: screen sharing.

Screen Sharing

While in either a voice or video call there is an option in the Sharing menu on the Call Management bar (Figure 5-16) to share your screen. You can share either the full screen or a selected window. Either party on a one-to-one Skype call or any participant on a group voice or video call can share his or her full desktop screen or a selected window within the desktop.

On selecting the Share your screen option a transparent pop up window appears (see Figure 5-26).

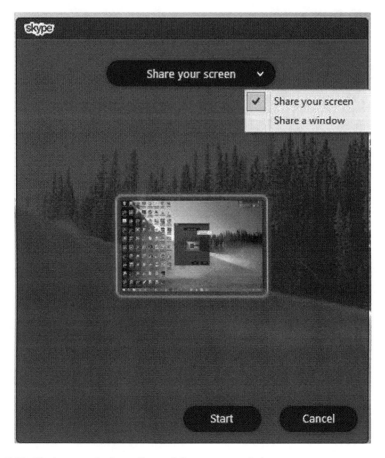

Figure 5-26. Start screen sharing options – full screen or a window

On selecting the Share a window option thumbnails of the various active windows appear on a transparent background (see Figure 5-27).

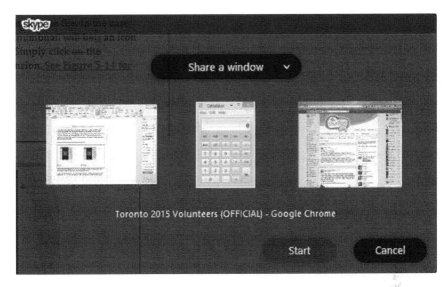

Figure 5-27. Select a window for screen sharing

Note that again it is a transparent window that cannot be moved from the center of the screen; as a result any content behind the background shows up faintly.

On selecting s particular window or the full screen, a red outline will appear around the window or full screen identifying it as the area of the desktop being shared (see Figure 5-28).

Figure 5-28. A red outline identifies the shared window

The call monitoring window also indicates that sharing is occurring by offering a Stop sharing option (see Figure 5-29).

Figure 5-29. Call monitoring window during screen sharing

The viewer has the option to go full screen using the same full screen icon shown earlier in Figure 5-16.

For my own activities Skype screen sharing has become a heavily used support tool for assisting others with demonstrating or using applications, including Skype itself.

> **Caution**   Keep in mind that screen sharing will show all the content selected whether full screen or only a window. Ensure there is no content being shared that you would want to be confidential. Also be aware that the recipient can use a screen capture program, such as SnagIt, to capture anything being shared.

Group Video Calling

Skype for Windows Desktop supports Group Video Calling (see Figure 5-30), with up to ten participants. It can also share one participant's desktop during a Skype Group Video Call. In the spring of 2014, Skype made Group Video Calling a free feature.

Figure 5-30. Group Video Call

For each participant connected through a Skype client, a Group Video Call takes advantage of Skype's SILK technology to provide crystal-clear audio. Participants can also be added to the call's voice stream from a PSTN phone (see Chapter 6 for more details); however, voice quality is limited to that of the participant's carrier network. Again the speaker is highlighted by a blue "halo" around his/her video or avatar. When a participant goes to another application during the call, the Call Monitor window appears showing the video image or avatar of the speaker; it changes the video image shown as speakers change.

Skype for Windows Options

Select Tools | Options from the Skype client's main menu to customize Skype according to your local desires and hardware. Beyond the General options shown in Figure 5-31, options are available for:

- **Privacy:** Allow calls and messages from anyone or only your Skype Contacts.

- **Notifications:** Select from several options when you want to see notification of an activity in the Windows tray.

- **Call Settings:** Allow calls from other than Skype Contacts, and set call forwarding numbers, voice messages, and video settings.

- **Instant Messaging settings:** Manage history (archiving), compact chat view, selecting folder for received files, SMS settings.

  - IM appearance provides font selection and switching between small and large emoticons.

- **Advance Settings:** Manage automatic Skype software updates, hotkey settings, and accessibility mode.

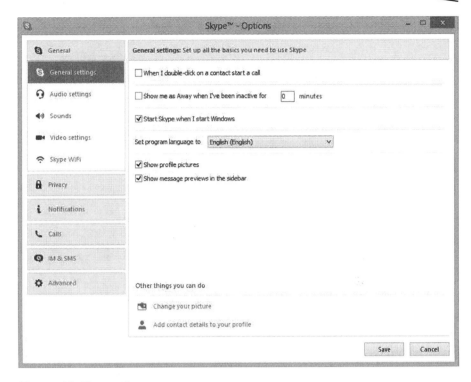

Figure 5-31. Skype options

Once you have experienced a few conversations and calls it is advised that you review these options to customize them to your individual privacy, activity, and hardware preferences.

SKYPE 7 FOR WINDOWS – DISPLAY OPTIONS

Skype 7 for |Windows comes with significant changes to the user interface. Many users have had issues with its increased use of white space and user profile images in both the Contacts pane and the conversation pane. The following options allow you to restore it to something close to its original appearance:

- View I Compact Sidebar View
- Tools I Options I IM & SMS ➤ uncheck Compact Chat View
- Tools I Options I IM & SMS I IM Appearance ➤ change font size
- Tools I General ➤ Uncheck Show profile pictures
- View I Split Window View

These settings allow you to customize the user interface experience to suit you.

Skype for Mac

Skype for Mac (OS X 10.5.8 and later) offers all the major communications features of Skype for Windows; however, the user interface has some significant differences from Skype for Windows Desktop. The most fundamental change is the use of the left and right panes, resulting in different user navigation for using a feature.

> **Note**   This discussion reflects the user experience in Skype 7.0 for Mac, released in October 2014.

Skype for Mac offers the same Home Page, Profile access, Contacts listings or directory and Conversation panes as found in Skype for Windows Desktop; however, they are accessed in a different way.

The overall user interface again has a left pane and right pane; however, the left pane simply acts as an index or sidebar menu.

The Index Pane

The Index pane provides access to the User Account Profile, Home Page, Contacts, Favorites, Recent Contacts, and a History option (Figure 5-32). The content associated with each of these items, including "directory" access to Contacts, appears in the right-hand pane.

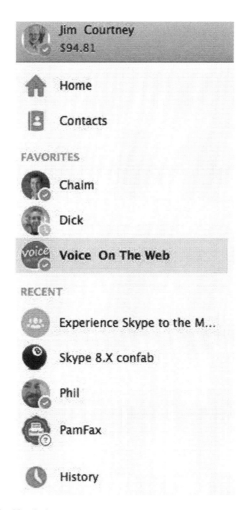

Figure 5-32. Skype for Mac Index pane

User's Skype Profile

Clicking on your Skype Name in the top-left corner brings up your Skype profile shown in Figure 5-33. This pane lets you edit your phone numbers, email addresses, and other fields. Note that there is no setting for time zone; this is picked up from the Mac's Date and Time settings.

Figure 5-33. Skype for Mac Skype profile

Contacts Directory or Listing

Clicking Contacts brings up a panel listing either all Contacts or subsets as determined by certain standard categories, or by Lists you created. If Contacts were originally set up with List assignments under Skype for Windows, they will carry over to Lists in Skype for Mac. In Figure 5-34, the All option lists all contacts, whether Skype, Facebook, or phone numbers only, while Online lists only those contacts who are currently online, and Skype lists only your Skype contacts. Not shown, but accessed via the >> button, is the Facebook option for accessing contacts added via Facebook. You can also access any other subset of Contacts that have been assigned to Lists in Skype for Windows.

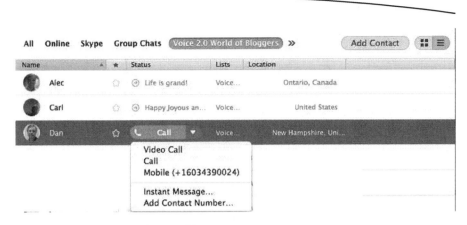

Figure 5-34. Skype for Mac Contacts Directory

In the left-hand sidebar (not shown), Recent lists only those Contacts with whom you have had a conversation either the same day or in the previous 24 hours, and History brings up a complete Conversation history in the right pane in reverse chronological order.

Skype Home Page

The Skype 7.0 for Mac Home page comprises the Contacts' most recent Mood Messages and/or your Facebook newsfeed. At the top you can enter or change your Mood Message. Figure 5-35 provides an example.

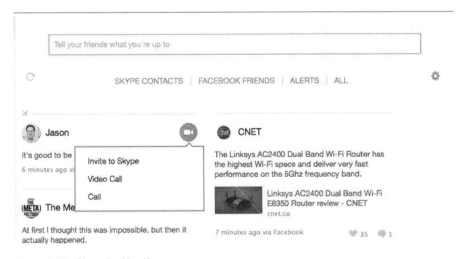

Figure 5-35. Skype for Mac Home page

The Window Menu

Skype for Mac includes a Window menu (see Figure 5-36) that provides access to separate windows in addition to the primary Skype conversation window. You can access the Dial Pad, a Contacts Monitor, Skype WiFi connections and Technical Call Info with this menu. The first three items are described here. The Technical Call Info Window provides diagnostic information about the call's performance.

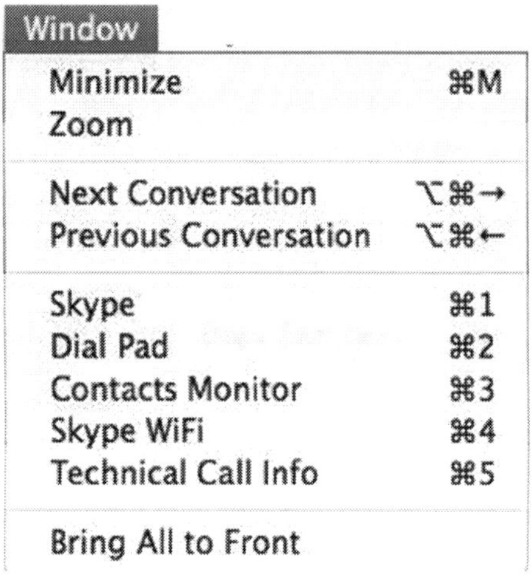

Figure 5-36. Skype for Mac Window menu

The Dial Pad (see Figure 5-37) allows entry of landline and mobile phone numbers to make a call and DTMF tones for working through interactive voice menus once a call is answered. It can also be accessed via the Dial Pad icon in the top bar of the Skype client.

Figure 5-37. Skype for Mac Dial Pad

The Contacts Monitor window (see Figure 5-38) provides a list of Contacts in a separate window. They can be filtered by a Group/List name.

Figure 5-38. Skype for Mac Home Contacts Monitor

The Skype WiFi menu shows any Skype WiFi access points available.

The Content Pane

The right pane's content depends on the items selected in the Index pane. For instance, as shown in Figure 5-39, select Contacts, search for a Contact in the top bar's Search entry and you see the various options for launching a conversation:

Figure 5-39. Skype for Mac Contact Search

Note that there are separate Contact listings for Skype and Facebook chat. Selecting a listed Contact opens a chat window with the ability to escalate the conversation to voice or video via the webcam and phone icons in the header. Within the Conversation pane's activity options (see Figure 5-40) you can:

- Launch a video or voice call

- Send files, a video message and/or a Contact profile

- Add People (for Group conversation)

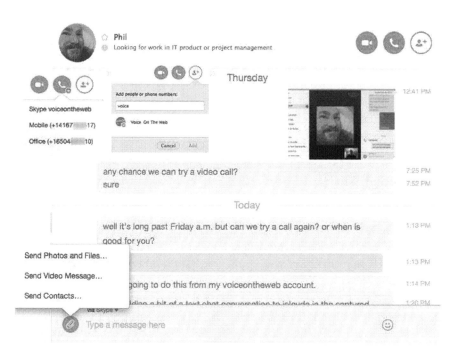

Figure 5-40. Skype for Mac Contact's Conversation Activity pane

Once a (chat, voice, or video) conversation has been initiated the Content pane contains the Conversation log, similar to what is seen in the Skype for Windows Conversation pane. It displays and records all chat conversation messages, file transfer activity, and call detail records for voice and video calls. Once again all the content is stored on the local PC and is searchable using Command-F. More information on using the Conversation pane, especially for chat, is covered in Chapter 8.

A Skype Voice Call

Launching a voice call brings up the dark background call screen with the Contact's Profile image and the Call Management bar (see Figure 5-41). The other party's name and time of the call appear in the upper-left corner. Clicking the double arrow in the upper-right corner expands the window to full screen.

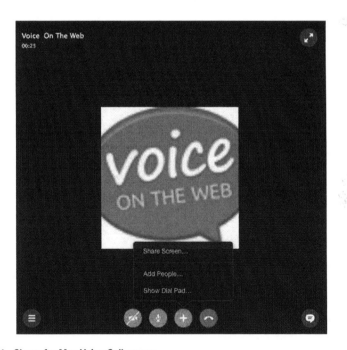

Figure 5-41. Skype for Mac Voice Call screen

Essential to managing the call is the Call Management bar at the bottom of the Call Screen (see Figure 5-42). If it has disappeared after showing for several seconds, click your mouse over the lower portion of the Call Screen to bring it back.

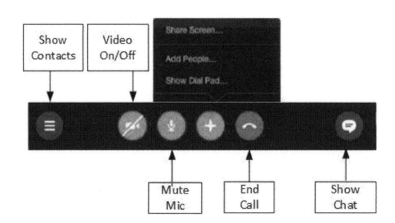

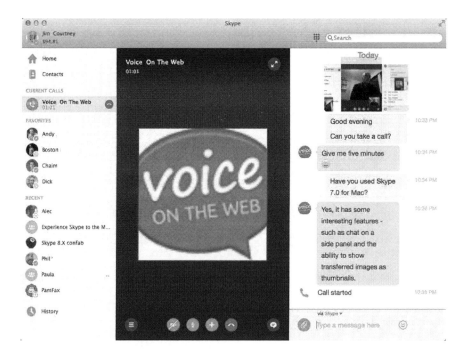

Figure 5-42. Skype for Mac Call Management bar

Again Skype for Mac does make it convenient to escalate a conversation from chat to voice to video. At any point screen sharing can also be invoked.

With Show Contacts and Show Chat invoked, the screen becomes a three-panel display (see Figure 5-43).

Figure 5-43. Skype for Mac three-panel call screen

By narrowing or widening the Skype window the chat is moved between a sidebar on the right side (wide) and a panel below the call screen (narrow) as shown in Figure 5-44.

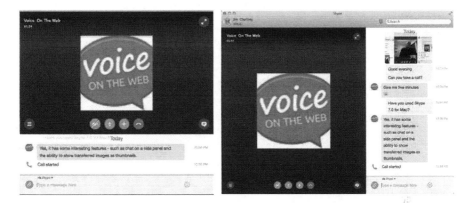

Figure 5-44. Skype for Mac chat panel with narrow (left) and wide (right) Skype client

There is no Call Quality Information bar as in Skype for Windows; however, from the Window menu (shown earlier in this section) one can access the Technical Call Info (see Figure 5-45). (Audio and Video settings are found in Skype | Preferences | Audio/Video.)

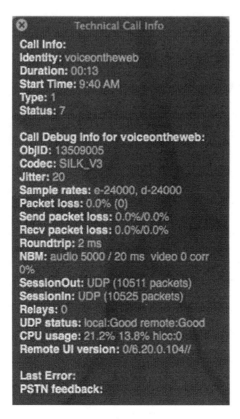

Figure 5-45. Skype for Mac Call Technical Info Window

If you change the cursor focus to another Mac application, a small Call Monitor window (see Figure 5-46) will appear on your desktop, with video if in a video call. From this window you can mute a mic and end the call.

Figure 5-46. Skype for Mac Voice Call Monitor window

A Skype Video Call

Either from the Contact toolbar or, if in a voice call, clicking the webcam button launches a video call. Most often video from the Mac comes using the built-in webcam at VGA resolution; however, if you have a Summer 2011 MacBook or Mac with the second generation Intel Core processor or later, Skype supports sending 720p HD resolution video.

Upon launching a call you will again get the Call screen but with the Contact's video in lieu of his/her avatar (see Figure 5-47).

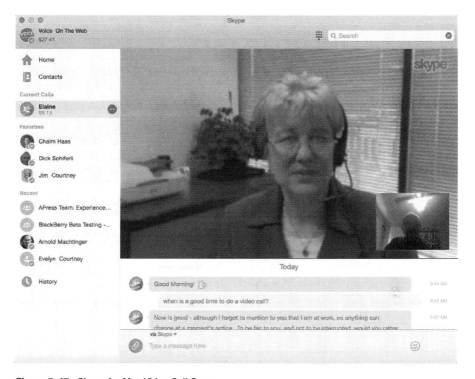

Figure 5-47. Skype for Mac Video Call Screen

The Call Management bar is the same as for a voice call, but with the webcam icon activated.

If you switch to another application during a call, the call monitor windows appears on the desktop incorporating a video image along with the ability to mute the mic and end the call (see Figure 5-48).

Figure 5-48. Skype for Mac Video Call Monitor

Skype for Mac also supports hosting of Group Video calls with up to ten participants and screen sharing by one of the participants.

In a call with a party on Skype for iPhone/iPad/Android, the Skype 7.0 for Mac (or later) call screen automatically rotates the video image on the Mac to avoid having the image go "sideways" when the other party rotates their mobile device.

> **Note**   Historically Skype for Mac lagged behind in features found on Skype for Windows but more recently they have become virtually feature equivalent. Features introduced on upgrades now occur on both platforms concurrently. While the user experience may have some differences, including implementation of some unique Mac OS X user interface features, the call experience itself is very similar.

More details on using Chat in business and participating in multi-party conversations will be covered in future chapters.

> **Tip**   If left unattended or even logged off for a while, many messages will pop up as unread when returning to Skype. However, you can easily mark all conversations as read (see Figure 5-49).

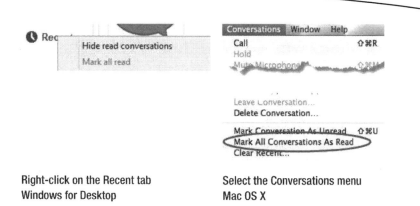

Right-click on the Recent tab   Select the Conversations menu
Windows for Desktop   Mac OS X

Figure 5-49. Mark All As Read

Skype for Mac Preferences

Select Skype | Preferences from the Skype client's main menu to customize Skype according to your local desires and hardware. Beyond the General options shown in Figure 5-50, options are available for:

- **Privacy:** Allow calls and messages from anyone or only your Skype Contacts.

- **Calls:** Allow calls from other than Skype Contacts, set call forwarding numbers, voice messages, and video settings.

- **Messaging:** Set SMS and emoticon features.

- **Notifications:** Select from several options when you want to see a Notification of an activity in the Windows tray.

- **Audio/Video:** Select mic, speakers, and webcam (default is the hardware embedded into a Mac).

- **Advance Settings:** Manage automatic Skype software updates, hotkey settings, and accessibility mode.

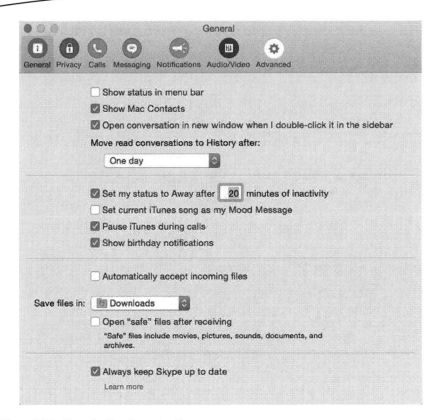

Figure 5-50. Skype for Mac General options

Once you have experienced a few conversations and calls, it is advised that you review these options to customize them to your individual privacy, activity, and hardware preferences.

Summary

This chapter provides a guide to the details of using Skype's key features in your real time and asynchronous communications activities on a Windows or Mac PC. One should take the time to check out all the options available while participating in conversations. Very quickly navigating through and participating in conversations should become intuitive. The biggest challenge is understanding how these features can be integrated into your business processes to facilitate overall productivity.

Key Points

■ The common Skype Home screen terminology provides access to Recent, Favorites, and People (Contacts).

■ Using Skype on a PC can archive conversations going back years; while Skype on a mobile device will, at most, archive conversations for up to 30 days.

■ The Skype Call Management bar on a PC, seen during a call, provides access to features such as file transfer, chat sessions, mic and speaker management, and the dial pad during a voice or video call. You can also add people to build a group call, share screens, hide/show contacts, and display the call full screen.

■ Options or preferences provide the flexibility to customize privacy, notification, hardware, and call handling settings to your individual choices.

■ See Chapter 6 for coverage of Skype for modern Windows, as this is a mobile-style interface, even when used on a desktop.

Using Skype on Mobile Devices

After experimenting with various attempts at using Skype on mobile phones, Skype launched a true Skype application on the iPhone in April 2009[1]. Initially, it only worked over Wi-Fi access points but you could call landline and mobile phone numbers from any Wi-Fi access point worldwide. Subsequent releases and upgrades for mobile devices have delivered:

- ▓ Support for use on wireless carrier networks (using data plans)

- ▓ Skype for Android, iPad, BlackBerry 10, Windows 8 tablets, Windows Phone 8, and Amazon Fire

- ▓ Fully featured chat, including support for SMS messages and edit/remove messages

- ▓ Integration with native contacts on a device

- ▓ Significant reductions in battery drain such that it is not an issue any longer

- ▓ HD video calling with high-quality images

- ▓ Support for Bluetooth audio and video shake compensation technology.

---

[1]http://voiceontheweb.biz/2009/04/skype-for-iphone-the-response-and-coverage/

- Bluetooth audio allows hands-free Skype calls to be made in suitably equipped vehicles (iOS and BlackBerry 10 only)

- A common user interface across most platforms

- Participation in Group conversations (text and voice; voice only in Group Video)

In September 2014, Skype for iPhone introduced two new features that will migrate to Skype on other mobile platforms:

- Ability to host a Group Voice call for up to four participants

- Answering a Skype call directly from the lock screen such that an incoming Skype call is treated like an incoming mobile phone call over a wireless carrier's voice channel

Let's start by looking at the Skype features available on the various mobile applications.

SKYPE FOR MOBILE ON WIRELESS CARRIERS

Skype's software is built using IP-based communications protocols. As a result Skype on any mobile device needs access to a data connection to the Internet, whether over a Wi-Fi access point or a wireless carrier. To minimize costs, recommendations include:

- Wherever possible use Wi-Fi for your Internet connection, especially when roaming outside your carrier's "home" territory.

- On the home carrier ensure a subscription includes a multi-GB data plan; the amount depends on expected usage of Skype over the carrier.

- When roaming and using a carrier, look for multi-carrier, multi-country service offerings, such as Truphone's World Plan, to minimize data plan costs.

Skype Features on Mobile Devices

Note   The following discussion covers iPhone, Android phones and tablets, BlackBerry 10 (which is a hybrid Android/BlackBerry 10 app), Windows 8 tablets, Windows Phone 8, and Amazon Fire. Skype for iPad's user interface is similar to Skype for Mac OS X.

Skype is an application available on the Apple App Store, Google Play, BlackBerry World, Amazon Appstore, and Windows Phone Store. Simply install it and log in to your Skype account (via either your Microsoft ID or Skype ID).

On smartphones and tablets, functionality is usually limited to:

- One-to-one voice and video calling
- Participation in multi-party calls
- Presence
- Text messaging
  - Chat, including Group Chat and SMS
- Conversation archiving (up to 30 days)
- Voice mail
- Video messaging
- File transfer
  - Photos only on iPhone and iPad

As mentioned before, all these features are free except calls to landline and mobile phone numbers (including participants on a multi-party call), SMS messaging and call forwarding to a landline or wireless number (call forwarding to another Skype user is free).

Now let's look at the various Skype screens seen on the mobile devices.

Navigating Skype Mobile Screens

A major difference between Skype on a PC and Skype on a mobile device is the need to navigate through multiple screens for accessing and participating in conversations due to the screen size. But there is a common starting point; across all devices the Home screen (see Figure 6-1) provides access to:

- Recent conversations, including Group Chats
- Favorites – frequently called contacts
  (see discussion in Chapter 5)
- People (Contacts)

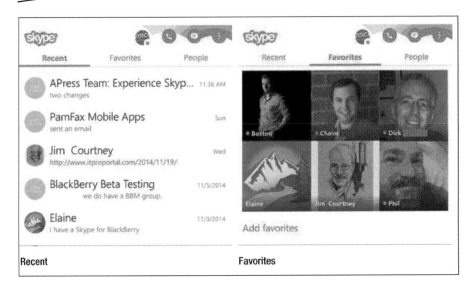

Figure 6-1. Skype on mobile Home screen

The People list can include (see Figure 6-2):

- Skype contacts
- All: Skype and native device contacts
- Available/Online contacts

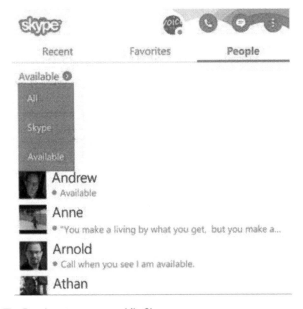

Figure 6-2. The People category on mobile Skype

Touch any Contact in any of these categories to start a conversation via the Chat screen. Across the different smartphone platforms the viewable content is determined by the screen size (see Figure 6-3), but there is a commonality of icons.

iPhone 5   BlackBerry Z30   BlackBerry Passport

Figure 6-3. Skype on various mobile screens

Tablets (with screen size greater than seven inches) show even more content within the display.

Below the text entry pane are navigation options from the conversation screen (see Figure 6-4):

- The message entry window and icon bar

- The Voice call options

- The three dot menu options

- The message entry window accepts text with the option to include emoticons in the message

- The + icon launches a file transfer (documents and photos). The paperclip on the iPhone launches photo sharing only.

- The telephone icon opens options for making a voice call, either via Skype or to landline or mobile phone numbers associated with the contact.

- The webcam icon launches a Skype video call to the contact.

- The three dot menu leads to options associated with Favorites and the contact's Skype profile.
  - On iPhone it also offers the option to Add Participants for a Group Chat or Voice Call, set notifications, and delete the Chat session history.
  - On Android/BlackBerry 10 it also provides for editing, blocking, or removing a contact.

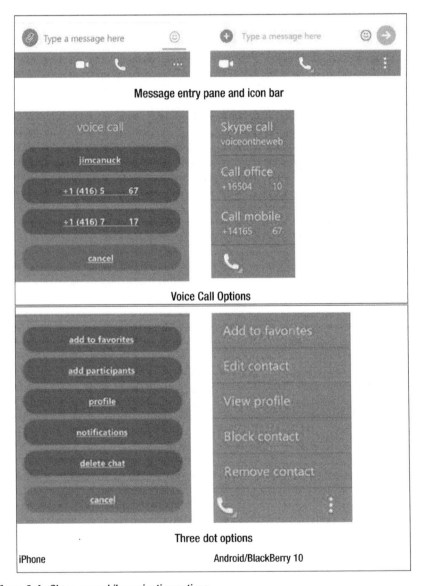

Figure 6-4. Skype on mobile navigation options

> **Note**   You can always return to the Home screen or previous screen
> using the left arrow at the top of each screen.

The Skype Home screens on mobile devices incorporate other icons that
can lead directly to launching a conversation (see Figure 6-5).

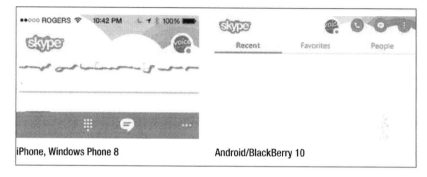

iPhone, Windows Phone 8   Android/BlackBerry 10

Figure 6-5. Skype on mobile conversation icons

▨   Selecting the phone/dial pad icon launches a dial pad.
    Note the small directory icon in the upper-right corner of
    the dial pad screen from which you can select a Contact
    and then a phone number.

▨   Selecting the cloud icon launches a chat session;
    however when launching these sessions you then need
    to select a contact.

Tapping on the Skype Profile image on the opening screen opens a screen
for managing the user's account (see Figure 6-6).

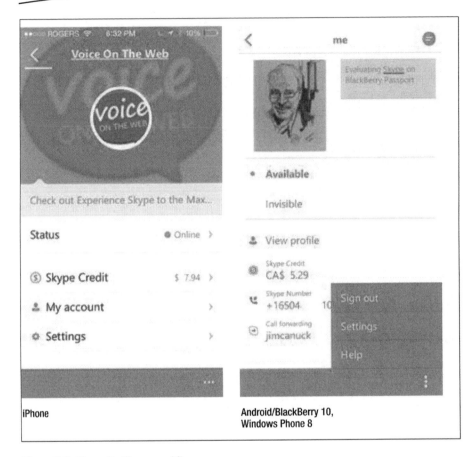

Figure 6-6. Skype Profiles on mobile

Now that we've seen how to navigate the interface, let's look at what happens when you want to make a Skype call from your mobile device.

Making a Voice Call on Mobile Devices

While chat remains the most used feature of Skype on mobile platforms, Skype is also very convenient for making voice and video calls at low cost.

As mentioned earlier, clicking on a phone icon launches a voice call, while clicking on a webcam icon launches a video call.

On placing or answering a voice call, one of three screens appears (see Figure 6-7).

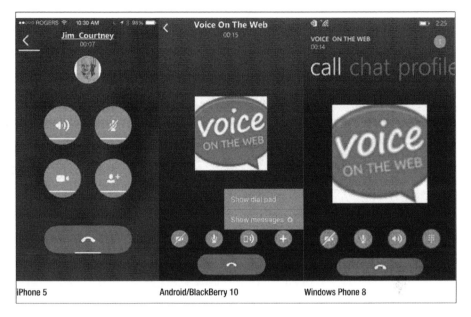

iPhone 5 | Android/BlackBerry 10 | Windows Phone 8

Figure 6-7. Skype on mobile voice call screens

The call management bar across the bottom of each screen manages:

- **Webcam:** This is an on/off button for the webcam and the toggle between rear and front camera. It initially opens with front camera (if available).

- **Mic mute:** Toggles the microphone on/off.

- **Speaker:** Switches between the internal and external speaker.

- **+ (Android/BlackBerry 10):** Accesses the dial pad or shows the Chat conversation screen.

- **Head "+" (iPhone only):** Add (up to three) contacts for a multi-party call.

- **Dial pad:** (Windows Phone 8 only): Accesses the dial pad.

There is no option to share a screen from any of these platforms, but it is possible to receive a screen share from another call participant who is calling from a PC.

> **Note** When viewing a shared screen on a mobile device, your screen size may limit how much detail you can see.

AN IMPROVEMENT TO THE MOBILE CALLING EXPERIENCE

Beyond echo cancellation and superwideband audio, one outstanding issue affecting the calling environment has been the background noise environment you're in when making or receiving a call, such as in an airport, train station, shopping mall, sports event, or concert hall. However, taking advantage of phones with multiple microphones, such as more recent Microsoft Lumia phones and the BlackBerry Passport, Skype has introduced audio processing technology such that when using Skype in these situations, signals from all the microphones are combined using the phone's inherent smart signal processing technology to zoom in to your voice and cancel everything else.

The Future of Mobile Skype

Over the past few years since the Microsoft acquisition, Skype has made it a priority to improve the mobile Skype experience, not only with crystal-clear audio and HD video but also improving the underlying infrastructure so that you can, for instance, keep your chat session content up to date, especially when you have been out of the Skype app for a while. New capabilities, such as the ability to view transferred photos within the conversation screen are coming. With automatic updates on these devices, you will always have the latest version installed.

Skype on mobile devices will soon become an alternative conversation service, replacing the legacy voice channel. This has evolved through the availability of:

- More robust and feature-rich software

- Evolution of a "cloud" environment for buffering messages and shared files/photos

- More powerful processors on newer devices

- Operating system upgrades that allow Skype to remain present in the background

Note   To enable Skype as a background application waiting for a chat message or call, simply open Skype and go to other applications. At this point Skype remains invisibly available to receive calls and provide message notifications when activity is triggered.

Summary

Skype functionality on mobile devices is limited, but improving all the time. With the ability to answer Skype calls directly from the lock screen on an iPhone (added September 2014), the calling experience increasingly resembles a normal mobile call, but with Skype's characteristic ability to enrich your conversations with features like chat and file and photo sharing.

The mobile Skype interface differs across devices, but has certain features in common that make it easier to find the functions you are looking for, no matter what device or combination of devices you are using.

Key Points

- Skype on mobile devices supports most Skype features with the exclusion of hosting group calls (except on iPhone) and long-term conversation archiving.

- The Skype Home screen on mobile devices follows the Recent, Favorites, People paradigm as the launch point for conversations.

- Skype provides a crystal-clear audio quality, overcoming the distorted voice quality of the mobile carrier's legacy voice channel.

- Skype on mobile devices requires the user to navigate through multiple screens to access all Skype's features on the smaller display of smartphones.

- Using Skype on a mobile device over a robust enough Wi-Fi connection provides a low cost or free means of placing international calls from hotels, airports, coffee shops, and conference center while traveling.

Chapter **7**

Calling and Messaging Landlines and Mobile Phones

While voice and video calls to other Skype users are free, Skype users also want to make voice calls with their family, friends, and business colleagues who do not have Skype access but do have conventional landline or mobile phone voice services. Many business operations also use Skype on their PC as their sole desktop phone, yet need an inbound number for receiving calls from suppliers, contractors, and customers. Skype offers not only services for outbound and inbound calling but also uses the same infrastructure to provide other low-cost calling features.

Connecting with the Legacy Phone Network

Skype has made available several ways to place and receive calls to/from landlines and mobile phones:

▨ **Calling landlines and mobile phones:** Outbound calling from a Skype client to landlines and mobile phones worldwide

▨ **Skype Numbers:** Inbound calling to a phone number that is answered on a Skype client

- **SMS Messaging:** Sending SMS messages to a mobile phone

- **Skype To Go:** Calls to local phone numbers that forward to landlines and mobile phones worldwide using Skype credit or a Skype Calling Plan subscription

Calling Phone Numbers Worldwide at Low Costs

"Calling phone numbers" refers to calls made from Skype to landlines and mobile phones worldwide. Skype has already negotiated arrangements with phone companies (carriers) in over 180 countries that result in rates as low as 2.3 cents per minute for calls to U.S., Canada, and most European countries.

Here are a few details associated with calling landlines and mobile phones:

- All offerings are "prepaid" using Skype Credit or a Skype Calling Plan subscription.

- Pay-as You-Go per minute calling rates[1] depend on the country and, in some cases, the carrier where the call is terminated.

- On Pay-as-You-Go calls, in addition to the per-minute charge there is a small per call connection fee[2] that varies by termination country.

- Skype Calling Plans are unlimited subscriptions to landlines in 63 countries and mobile phones in 8 of those 63 countries.

Skype Calling Plan minutes can also be applied to:

- Each leg of a Skype multi-party call where the participant is connected through a landline or mobile phone.

- Call forwarding a Skype call to a landline or mobile number.

This chapter starts out by discussing the various prepaid payment programs available for placing and receiving calls to/from landlines and mobile phones. The discussion continues with examples of using the various services described previously.

---

[1]http://www.skype.com/intl/en/prices/payg-rates/?currency=USD#viewAllRates.
[2]http://www.skype.com/intl/en-us/prices/payg-rates/connection-fees/.

The Skype Account

As there are charges associated with these calls, Skype offers several programs for using these services. Initiating and managing them is provided through your Skype Account on the Skype website. Simply go to www.skype.com and sign in via the button on the upper right.

The following discussion covers the Skype Account as it relates to calling landlines and mobile phones (Figure 7-1). A more extensive outline of the full Skype Account management is covered in Chapter 9, including managing payment options.

Figure 7-1. Managing Skype features

Note   You'll never get a phone bill with Skype!

Calls to and from landlines and mobile phones may be prepaid through:

- A Pay-as You-Go basis, using prepaid Skype Credit[3]

- A monthly, quarterly, or full year Skype Calling Plan subscription[4]

- A Skype Number[5] subscription

---

[3]http://www.skype.com/intl/en-us/prices/skype-credit/.
[4]http://www.skype.com/intl/en/prices/pay-monthly/.
[5]http://www.skype.com/intl/en/features/allfeatures/online-number/.

Skype Credit

Skype Credit is used for Pay-As-You-Go to cover:

- Calls to landline and mobile numbers without a subscription

- Skype Online Numbers

- Skype To Go

- Call forwarding to a landline or mobile phone

- Skype WiFi

- SMS Messaging

Skype credit may be purchased by signing into your Skype account on the Skype website or via links on the Skype Profile screen on mobile devices.

Alternatively, you can set up a Skype Calling Plan subscription that covers these services at fixed costs.

CALLS TO MOBILE PHONES

In most countries worldwide calls to mobile phones are "caller pays." As a result, outbound calls to mobile phones in these countries can have rates ranging from $.10 per minute to over $.50 per minute. They use Skype Credit and are not included in Skype Calling Plan subscriptions. As of March 2015 calls to mobile phones in U.S., Canada, China, Singapore, Hong Kong, Thailand, Puerto Rico, and Guam are included in a Skype Calling Plan subscription.

Skype's Calling Plan Subscriptions

Skype has established flat-rate subscriptions that provide unlimited calling to a designated geographical region, within the limits of their Fair Usage policy. Skype Calling Plan subscriptions:

- Provide flat-rate unlimited calling to landline and mobile phones:

  - Unlimited Country: Within your home country code

  - Unlimited Continent: Within a continent (North America and Europe)

  - Unlimited World: Worldwide to over 60 countries

■ Offer options to purchase 60-, 120-, or 400-minute monthly bundles for calls within the local country (available in select countries)

■ Offer a 50% discount on one Skype Online number with a 12-month subscription

■ Include call forwarding to a phone number

The Unlimited World Plan coverage includes 8 countries to landlines and mobile phones and 55 countries to landlines only (see Figure 7-2).

Figure 7-2. Skype Calling Plan subscription countries

SKYPE WORLD PLAN SPECIAL OFFERS

As Skype is integrated into Microsoft's other products, such as Office 365, special offers are becoming available for Skype World calling:

- Sign up for a Skype Unlimited World subscription and get the first month free with no obligation to continue after the free month.

- Office 365 subscribers get 60 free World calling minutes per month with their Office 365 subscription.

For example, for Skype users in the U.S. and Canada (country code 1) there are three options available:[6]

- **Unlimited U.S. and Canada:** $2.99/month

- **Unlimited North America:** $7.99/month (adds landlines to three cities in Mexico; Mexico City, Guadalajara, and Monterrey)

- **Unlimited World:** $13.99/month (adds calls to all 60+ countries shown in Figure 7-2)

From Skype.com's main navigation bar select Prices ➤ Rates[7] and select a destination country for more details on an individual country basis. A 15% discount applies to a 12-month subscription.

Set up a Skype Calling Plan subscription via the Prices ➤ Rates menu on the Skype.com home page or via My Account on the Skype website.

Calling Landlines and Mobile Phones

While the dial pad (see Figure 7-3) is available to manually launch calls to landline and mobile phones, calls can also be initiated by clicking or tapping on:

- Phone number entries in People in Office 365, especially Outlook 2013

- Phone number entries in a mobile device's People directory on the Home Screen of Skype's mobile applications; it incorporates contacts in the device's native Contacts

---

[6]http://www.skype.com/intl/en-us/prices/pay-monthly/.
[7]http://www.skype.com/intl/en-us/prices/.

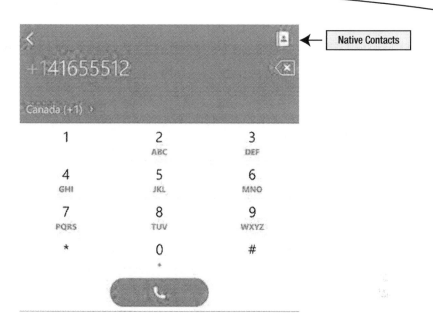

Figure 7-3. Skype on mobile dial pad

Having entered or selected a phone number, from a Contacts directory click the phone icon to launch a call. Once answered, you see the voice call screen described in the following section.

The Phone Number Voice Call Screen

When making a call to a landline or mobile phone number there are two options on the Call Management Bar for calls using either a PC or Mac (see Figure 7-4) or mobile device (see Figure 7-5):

- A Dial Pad icon, to interact with interactive voice menus

- Chat offers to send an SMS message

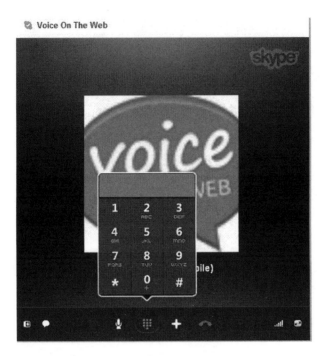

Figure 7-4. Dial pad on landline and mobile phone calls from a PC

Figure 7-5. Voice Call screens on smartphones and tablets

CALLER ID

When placing a call to landlines and mobile phones, Skype sends a caller ID with either your SkypeID or the anonymous 0123456.

However, you can set your caller ID to be one of two numbers:

- A mobile phone number registered in your Skype profile
- A Skype Online number

To set the caller ID, log in to your Skype Account on Skype.com and select Caller ID from the Manage Features bar (see Figure 7-6). Note that, where you have both a mobile number and Skype number(s), there is the option to have the displayed caller ID be a local number to the place you are calling.

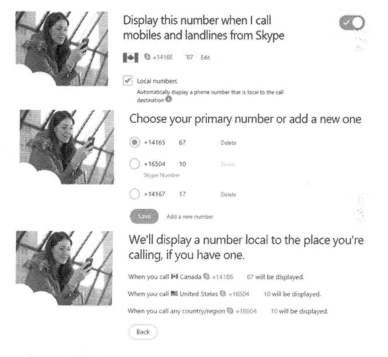

Figure 7-6. Selecting a Caller ID

Skype Numbers: "Local" Numbers with Worldwide Reach

A Skype Number allows Skype users to receive calls from landlines and mobile phones on their Skype client wherever it may be open worldwide.

- A landline or mobile phone call to a Skype online phone number can be answered on your PC, smartphone, tablet, TV, or other Skype-enabled devices.

- Skype Online Numbers are available for 24 countries (see Figure 7-7)

  - In Germany you must be a German resident to have a German Skype number

- A Skype account can be associated with up to ten Skype Numbers; such that one can have a "local" U.S., U.K., and France number.

- Skype Numbers for business use can be provisioned with Skype Manager.

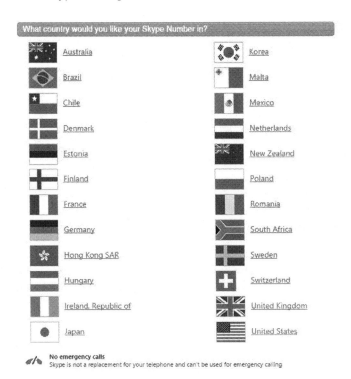

Figure 7-7. Skype Number countries

A most common consumer application of Skype Online numbers is to provide "free" calling to expats living on another continent. For instance a U.S. citizen living in Europe can have his family call a U.S. Skype Online number for calls that will be received on their Skype client wherever they are in Europe. In fact, with call forwarding calls can be then be forwarded to a mobile phone at outbound calling rates, if the call is not answered using Skype.

The countries shown in Figure 7-7 are current as of February 2015 and may change at Skype's discretion.

Set up personal Skype Numbers via the Skype Number tab on your Skype Account page.

FAIR USAGE POLICY

Skype subscriptions are designed for consumer and small business calling worldwide. As a result there are some restrictions on their use in a business. These restrictions include:

- Using subscriptions for telemarketing or call center operations

- Re-selling subscription minutes

- Sharing subscriptions between users whether via a PBX, call center, computer, or any other means

- Calling numbers (whether singly, sequentially, or automatically) to generate income for yourself or others as a result of placing the call, other than for your individual business communications (and subject to Section 4.1 of the Terms of Use);

- Unusual calling patterns inconsistent with normal, individual subscription use; for example, regular calls of short duration or calls to multiple numbers in a short period of time.

Skype reserves the right to change these restrictions at its discretion.

SMS Messaging

Skype's SMS Messaging[8] allows you to send text messages from your Skype chat window to mobile phones worldwide. SMS Messaging rates[9] start as low as $0.05 per message; they are based on the destination country of the message and tend to be in the $0.10 +/-$0.02 per message range for U.S., Canada, U.K., and most European countries.

---

[8]http://www.skype.com/intl/en/features/allfeatures/sms/.
[9]http://www.skype.com/intl/en/prices/sms-rates/#viewAllRates.

Note that for some countries SMS messaging may only be one way from Skype to the mobile phone. Figure 7-8 is an example in which the Canadian SMS message service will not forward SMS messages to Skype. In this case it is considered to provide notification rather than support true conversations that can be carried on via true SMS. An alternative is to converse by chat using Skype for iPhone, Android, BlackBerry 10, or Windows Phone.

Figure 7-8. SMS messaging is outbound only

Skype To Go

Skype To Go[10] is a Skype feature, available in 24 countries, which allows a Skype user to assign a "local" phone number to as many as 30 designated contacts worldwide (Figure 7-9). As a result, provided you are within your "local" calling region, landline and mobile calls can be made to these 30 contacts using either Skype Credits or a Skype Calling Plan subscription. The called party answers the call on their remote landline or mobile phone.

---

[10]http://www.skype.com/intl/en/features/allfeatures/skype-to-go-number/.

Figure 7-9. Skype To Go numbers

For example, on my Skype To Go plan[11], there are nine "local" +1 (647) numbers that forward calls out to contacts in Canada, U.S., U.K., Hong Kong, and South Africa at the cost of a local landline or wireless call, since a Skype Calling Plan subscription comes into play. Basically Skype To Go has become a plan for making low-cost international long distance calls from a landline or mobile phone within the user's "home" territory to a designated contact's landline or mobile phone.

Skype To Go is especially useful for making calls to these designated contacts from a mobile phone when in your mobile phone's "home" territory. On mobile devices the call does go out over your carrier's voice channel, whereas Skype-to-Skype calls go over the carrier's data channel. On all devices these calls use Skype Credit or a Skype Calling Plan subscription.

Skype To Go is set up via the tab of the same name on your Skype Account page. The countries supported in February 2015 are shown in Table 7-1 and may change at Skype's discretion.

Table 7-1. Countries Supported by Skype To Go

Australia	Ireland	Romania
Canada	Latvia	Slovenia
Chile	Lithuania	Singapore
Denmark	Luxembourg	South Africa
Estonia	Mexico	Sweden
Finland	New Zealand	Taiwan
Greece	Poland	United Kingdom
Hungary	Portugal	USA

---

[11]http://voiceontheweb.biz/2010/11/skype-to-go-becoming-my-first-choice-wireless-long-distance-service/.

Click-to-Call

When you install Skype for Windows you have the option to install a browser plug-in called Click-to-Call. Click-to-Call[12] scans a web page as you load it and enables landline or mobile phone calling to any phone numbers found on the web page.

You can administer Click-to-Call by clicking the Skype icon found in the browser toolbar (see Figure 7-11). clicking the Skype logo in any of Chrome, Firefox, and Internet Explorer gives the option shown in Figure 7-10.

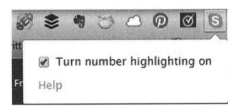

Figure 7-10. Click-to-Call browser toolbar button

When number highlighting is turned on, a phone number found on a web page is highlighted with Skype's Click-to-Call icon comprising the phone number and a Skype logo. Click the number to launch a SkypeOut call to the number. Mouse over the number to get the Call / Add to Skype menu.

Figure 7-11. Click-to-Call navigation

Click-to-Call does require that you have Skype credit or a Skype Calling Plan subscription. However, businesses can register as an advertiser[13] with Skype such that a Click-to-Call button always appears on the advertiser's web page, allowing the web page visitor to make a free landline call to the advertiser.

---

[12]http://www.skype.com/intl/en/get-skype/on-your-computer/click-to-call/.
[13]http://www.skype.com/intl/en/advertise/click-to-call/.

Click-to-Call is an extension in the various browsers and will often offer updates within the browser independent of updates to Skype for Windows.

Summary

Skype offers several services that bridge calls to the legacy telephone network of landline and mobile phones. Outbound calling to landlines and mobile phones is available to over 200 countries. A Skype account can add Skype Online number(s) for inbound calling to a user's Skype activities, and SMS messages can be sent to wireless phones.

Key Points

Calling to any landline or mobile phone worldwide from a PC can happen at low cost. But there are notable use cases for the various landline and mobile phone offerings that can bring significant savings:

- **Outbound calling from Skype:** Calling any number worldwide from any geographical location worldwide with appropriate Wi-Fi or wired Ethernet Internet access (hotels, airports, restaurants, coffee shops, etc.)

- When Wi-Fi access is available calling to landlines and mobile phones using Skype is a low-cost alternative to carrier-supported mobile phone voice calls for calling relatives or business colleagues from any Skype-supported smartphone or tablet. This avoids wireless carrier roaming charges.

- **Skype Number:** Providing a "local" number in the traveler's home country which relatives, friends, and business colleagues can call while traveling internationally.

- **Caller ID:** Select either your registered mobile phone number or Skype Number.

- **Skype To Go:** Make calls at Skype's low costs to landlines and mobile phones from your mobile phone while traveling within your "Home" territory.

- **SMS Messaging:** Sending (but not receiving) SMS messages as an alternative to carriers' roaming SMS messaging.

Chapter 8

Skype Chat: A Virtual Water Fountain

While Skype has built its reputation for making free voice and video calls, Skype's chat feature changes how and why we carry out conversations. Since 2007 Skype Chat has become one of my primary communication services–on both PCs and mobile devices. This chapter builds from those experiences, whether working with clients operating worldwide or having ad hoc occasional conversations with both business and personal acquaintances from Germany to Australia.

With the recent changes to Skype's underlying support infrastructure, Chat opens up the ability to support asynchronous ad hoc or spontaneous dialogue–where both parties do not need to be "online" concurrently in order to exchange thoughts, ideas, and responses.

Why Chat?

As a business communications tool, chat provides the largest opportunity for enhancing productivity, especially across a geographically dispersed business's ecosystem:

- Conversations can be followed and tracked whether in the home office or on the road across PCs, smartphones, and tablets.

- Chat messages leave an archival record of conversations for later search and recall, going back years on PCs or up to 30 days on mobile devices.

- Chat opens up a new etiquette for starting voice or video conversations by checking whether other parties are available for a call. In a business environment it is considered responsible etiquette to use Skype chat to determine if another party is available and only call at an agreed on time, whether immediately, in five minutes, or five hours.

- Chat exchanges minimize the need to start a conversation with pleasantries such as "How's the weather?" or providing an update on personal life.

- Multiple chat threads can be followed concurrently.

- Chat supports ad hoc activity. Sustainable group chat sessions become virtual water fountain conversations in which participants make contributions and comments on an ad hoc basis.

- Chat allows a quick Yes/No/Maybe response to questions that require a simple clarification.

- Chat provides a home for a searchable "notebook," archiving meeting agendas and discussion notes while sharing website URLs, document files, photos, and contact information.

The Conversation Pane

The Conversation pane, on the right side of the Windows Desktop or Mac client, builds a persistent archive of all your Skype activity with each individual contact and group. When you select a contact, the Conversation pane:

- Includes a dialog box at the bottom for text and emoticon entry (along with a menu–via the paperclip icon–for sharing files, photos, and Skype contacts, and leaving video messages).

- Stores and recalls conversation history by Contact or Group going back in time.

- Records voice and video call details, including time of call, duration of call (Call Detail Records).

- Records file sharing activity with an active link to both the file and the folder in which it was stored.

■ Converts any entered website URL and email address to an active link.

■ Permits editing or removal of a message for up to an hour after it has been posted.

Text messages and other information are recorded with the most recent item at the bottom of the window. Note there is a time associated with each entry; if you scroll up you will also find date dividers.

In Skype for Windows the Conversation pane can be optionally split off as a separate window using the View | Split Window View menu selection (see Figure 8-1). This way you can have a separate window for each Contact's chat session or each Group Chat activity.

Figure 8-1. Compact View–separate Windows for separate chats

When you go to this mode double-click on a Contact's name in the Contact pane (now a separate window) and a new window opens up with that Contact's conversation log. It is probably best to do this when you have a second display on which you can display just those chat sessions.

Return to the single window view via View | Default View.

Figure 8-2 illustrates the various features of the Conversation pane.

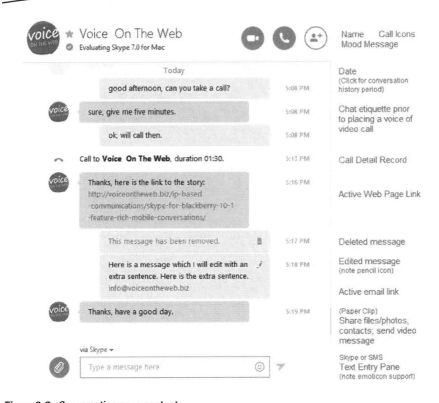

Figure 8-2. Conversation pane content

Figure 8-3 demonstrates both document and photo file sharing activity. Click the image to go to the document or open a default photo/graphics application. In the transition to buffering transferred files onto the Skype cloud, URLs may appear in lieu of these images.

Figure 8-3. The Conversation pane–file sharing

Within the Conversation pane there are several additional features:

■ How far back do you want to display the Conversation history content? Scroll to the top of the conversation pane, click Today or any date divider and select a time period (see Figure 8-4).

Figure 8-4. Restoring Conversation pane content

▨ You can search content to, say, retrieve URLs, meeting minutes, agendas, or any other word or phrase recorded into the Conversation history. A simple Ctrl-F (Command-F on Mac) opens the search window (see Figure 8-5). This is where Skype chat is a valuable productivity tool for accurately recording and later retrieving spellings, website or FTP URLs, or email addresses and contact information, amongst other content that can have later value.

Figure 8-5. Search the conversation history

▨ You don't need to miss messages simply because you have been offline. If you are using the most recent Skype updates, any messages entered by a contact while you were offline are stored by Skype and displayed in your Conversation pane when you next log in. Messages are stored for up to 30 days. Stored messages are even synchronized across multiple PCs and mobile devices should you log in to Skype on a different PC or device.

Need to copy, edit, or remove a message? Right-click a message and a menu with several options appears (see Figure 8-6).

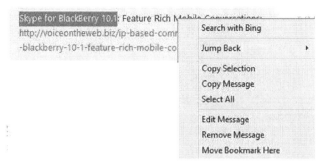

Figure 8-6. Right-click a message and a menu appears

▧ For up to an hour after you enter a message you can edit
or remove a message. However there are other options
in this menu that are available beyond the first hour:

▧ **Copy Message:** Copy the individual message to
the clipboard; you then have the option to paste the
copied message into the chat windows (optionally,
say, into a session with another contact or group chat)
either as a quote or text (see Figure 8-7).

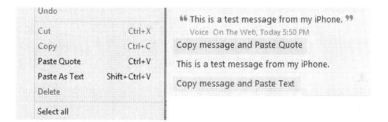

Figure 8-7. Paste options

▧ **Copy Selection or Select All:** Highlight multiple
or all messages in a thread and copy them to the
clipboard; they can then be copied as text only
into another chat entry window or pasted into any
document available via your desktop.

▧ **Search for Bing:** does a Bing search on any text
highlighted in the message.

Skype chat conversations and associated content concurrently appear across the various platforms with Skype clients and applications.

▦ A conversation can be followed on a Windows or Mac PC as well as an iPhone/iPod, an iPad, an Android smart device, a BlackBerry 10 phone, and a Windows Phone.

▦ There is never any indication which platform a contact is using; it's not needed. The user interface may be different on each; however, the chat content is consistent.

Warning   Your Skype chat history is only stored locally on your PC. If you move to a new PC or reinstall your operating system, you should back up the data prior to making the change.

On a Windows PC the chat history is found at C:\Users\[Windows User Name]\AppData \Roaming\Skype\[SkypeID] and can be copied to the same location after installing Skype on the new or reinstalled PC. On a Mac this is in ~/Library/Application Support/Skype/ [user name]/ and you need to copy the main.db file after first running Skype on a new Mac.

Chat Commands

Skype Chat also has a set of chat slash (/) commands that can be used within any version of Skype to manage chat activity. The most commonly used is /alertsoff, which stops those annoying sounds whenever someone logs on to Skype or enters a new message. The /me [text] command also gets a lot of use, especially in Group Chats. To get a list of commands type /help into the text entry pane and you will see what is shown in Figure 8-8.

System
Available commands: 11:53 AM
/me [text]
/add [skypename +]
/alertson [text]
/alertsoff
/help
For more help please see http://www.skype.com/go/help.chathelp

Figure 8-8. Chat slash / commands via /help

Clicking on the link at the end takes you to "What are chat commands and their roles?[1]" on the Skype website where you can obtain a complete list of available chat (/) commands. On that page you find instructions for determining whether a group chat is cloud-based or P2P-based along with two different sets of commands (see Figure 8-9):

Cloud-based chat commands and roles
P2P-based chat commands and roles

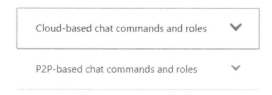

***Figure 8-9.** Chat commands and roles–two versions*

All one-to-one chat sessions are now cloud based; older *group* chats (before early 2013) are P2P based. Group chat options are discussed in Chapter 9.

For one-to-one chat sessions several of these commands can be useful while chatting:

- `/alertsoff` disables the audio message alert notification whenever someone adds a message to a session.
- `/me [text]` allows you to enter a comment that starts with your name followed by the text you enter (see Figure 8-10).

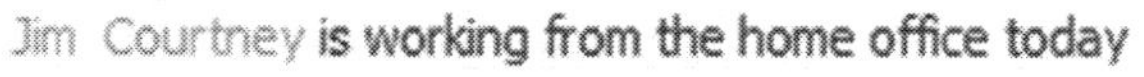

Jim Courtney is working from the home office today

***Figure 8-10.** "/me" Example*

- `/add [skypename]` adds another Skype contact to the chat session.
- `/showplaces` returns and identifies all the devices on which a particular Skype account is open (see Figure 8-11).

[1]https://support.skype.com/en-us/faq/FA10042/What-are-chat-commands-and-roles

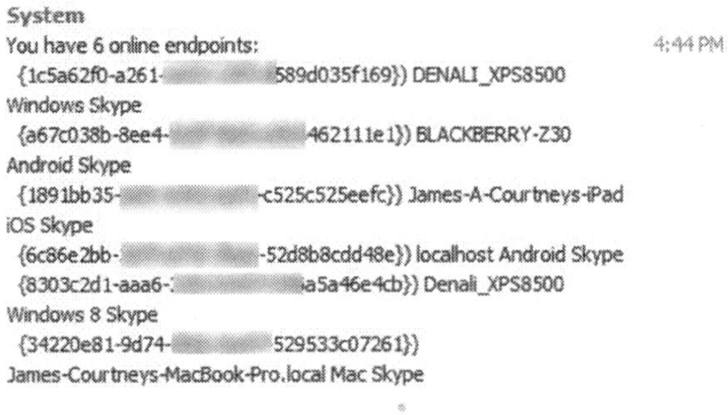

System
You have 6 online endpoints: 4:44 PM
    {1c5a62f0-a261-   589d035f169}) DENALI_XPS8500
Windows Skype
    {a67c038b-8ee4-   462111e1}) BLACKBERRY-Z30
Android Skype
    {1891bb35-   -c525c525eefc}) James-A-Courtneys-iPad
iOS Skype
    {6c86e2bb-   -52d8b8cdd48e}) localhost Android Skype
    {8303c2d1-aaa6-   a5a46e4cb}) Denali_XPS8500
Windows 8 Skype
    {34220e81-9d74-   529533c07261})
James-Courtneys-MacBook-Pro.local Mac Skype

Figure 8-11. Concurrent Skype online devices

Emoticons

A unique feature of Skype Chat is the large set of emoticons available for graphically expressing not only "facial" emotions but also illustration of other gestures, such as handshakes and dancing (see Figure 8-12). In fact, Skype has taken this one step further with graphics representing objects such as a birthday cake, a cup of coffee, and a dynamic "dancing" icon.

Figure 8-12. Skype Chat emoticons

Access the emoticons via the small emoticon icon at the right end of the Chat text entry window. On a PC scroll over the images to see what each represents as shown in the bottom status bar along with the character representation of the emoticon. In the example above, sweating is represented by (:|. On mobile apps, simply tap the desired icon.

Finally, there is a "hidden" range of rather expressive emoticons that have become favorites (or otherwise) over time as shown in Figure 8-13, including a working from home emoticon (wfh). To insert one you need to enter the character code within a pair of brackets. Using the ISO standard abbreviations for a country's name, you can create a flag icon using (flag:%%) where %% is the country's ISO code to obtain an appropriate flag graphic.

Figure 8-13. *Expressive emoticons*

As for the others, it is necessary to enter the associated text (Table 8-1); note that several of these emoticons are dynamic with a repetitive change over a few seconds.

Table 8-1. "Hidden" emoticon shortcuts

Text	Expression
(swear)	Swearing
(headbang) (banghead)	Banging head on wall
(drunk)	Drunk
(poolparty)	Pool Party
(rock)	Rock
(smoking) (smoke) (ci)	Smoking
(bug)	Bug
(e) (m) (mail)	You have mail
(o) (O) (time) (clock)	Time
(~) (film) (movie)	Movie
(skype) (ss)	Skype
(talk)	Talking
(call)	Call
(punch)	Punch
(u) (U) (brokenheart)	Broken heart
(mooning)	Mooning
(wfh)	Working from home
(flag:%%) e.g. (flag:ca)	Flag

Facebook Chat

As mentioned earlier, if you have connected a Skype for Windows Desktop or Skype for Mac client with your Facebook account, a completely independent set of contacts will show up in your Contacts pane, accessed through the Facebook tab. If you select to have a Facebook chat session the contact's name at the top of the Conversation pane will have "Facebook" under the Contact's name (see Figure 8-14).

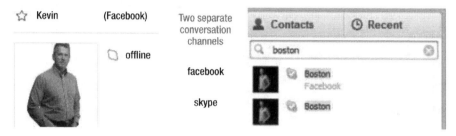

Figure 8-14. Facebook chat

The conversation itself is accessible also on other Facebook-supported platforms such as iPhone, iPad, Android, BlackBerry 10, and Windows Phone. Also keep in mind that Skype chat message content and Facebook chat message content comprise two fully independent message threads. Facebook message threads are archived on the local PC and searchable.

Summary

Chat has become perhaps the primary communications feature of Skype; it allows for asynchronous conversations across all platforms supported by Skype. It also provides searchable logging and archiving that records not only chat conversations but also call detail records, file transfer information, and clickable URLs.

Key Points

■ When fully implemented, chat becomes a productivity enhancement tool working across a business's entire ecosystem.

■ The Conversation pane on Skype for PCs or Conversation screen in Skype on mobile devices logs all activity amongst the chat participants: text messages, file transfer, call detail records, etc.

- Right-clicking a message in the PC or Mac client lets you copy, edit, or remove a message or selection of messages. Tapping and holding on a message on a mobile device will bring up a menu with the same options.

- The chat slash "/" commands provide management of the chat infrastructure: participants, notifications, roles, topics, as well as providing information such as all the devices logged in to a Skype account and number of participants in a group chat.

- Emoticons bring graphic expression to message content along with a participant's moods and feelings.

- If you have chosen to connect your Skype to your Facebook, you can use your Skype client on a Windows desktop or Mac to chat to your Facebook contacts.

- "Ctrl-F" on PC's or "Cmd-F" on Macs opens a search window to find archived content.

Chapter 9

Managing Your Skype Account and Subscriptions

In Chapter 7 the discussion included mention of your Skype Account as it relates to setting up various services, such as Calling Plan subscriptions when calling landlines and mobile phones. However, the Skype Account goes beyond managing these services to include managing your Skype profile and password, handling payments, and reviewing your Skype activity. Skype Manager also can manage Skype activity across a business or organization.

Pay in Advance—No Phone Bills

Skype's services for calling landline and mobile phones are Skype's major revenue source. Managing customer accounts, especially receivables, has always been a major logistics overhead and expense for the legacy landline and wireless phone companies.

Skype has avoided the significant overhead and expenses for generating and collecting revenue by setting up an account management infrastructure that:

▓ Requires payment in advance via a credit card or PayPal.

▓ Only allows access to an offering with prepaid Skype credit or subscriptions

▪ Has no collections requirements

▪ Reports on outbound calling details

▪ Takes measures to address security issues associated with using credit cards

▪ Sends no bills (although it does send out reminder emails when subscriptions are about to expire or Skype credit runs low)

The bottom line: With Skype you will never receive a phone bill—no surprises! You're in control. Now let's turn to how you manage your Account activities.

Managing Your Account

Individual users can manage their Skype Account by

▪ Navigating directly to the My Account page on the Skype website

▪ Selecting Manage my Account, accessed by clicking on your name in Skype for Windows Desktop or Skype for Mac button in a Skype client.

▪ Tapping on your Skype profile image on a touch screen mobile phone or tablet

If on a Windows PC or Mac OS X, sign in to your account and the My Account web page shown in Figure 9-1 comes up.

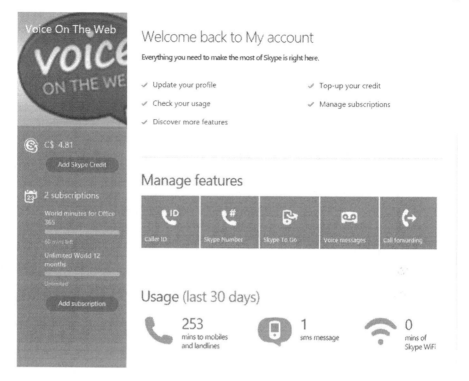

Figure 9-1. My Account web-based Skype portal

From this screen you can:

- Buy Skype credit
- Purchase Skype Calling Plan subscriptions
- Set up caller ID for use with SkypeOut calls
- Purchase a Skype number
- Set up Skype to Go numbers
- Enable Skype voice messages
- Set up call forwarding
- View usage: your outbound calling and SMS text messaging history

The details behind the landline and mobile phone services mentioned here are outlined in Chapter 7.

> **Note**   for security and fraud prevention reasons a credit card number can only be associated with a single Skype account. Using the Skype Manager (discussed later in this chapter), businesses can allocate Skype Credits to employees' business Skype accounts from a "master" Skype Manager account. The Skype Manager account would be associated with the user account used to log in to Skype Manager

On mobile devices, touch your Skype profile image on the home screen and various options related to managing your account will appear. If you select Skype Credit you will then be offered options to buy either a Subscription or Skype Credit.

But there's more to managing your Skype account. You can check out details behind use of your account (see Figure 9-2) by scrolling down on the screen shown in Figure 9-1.

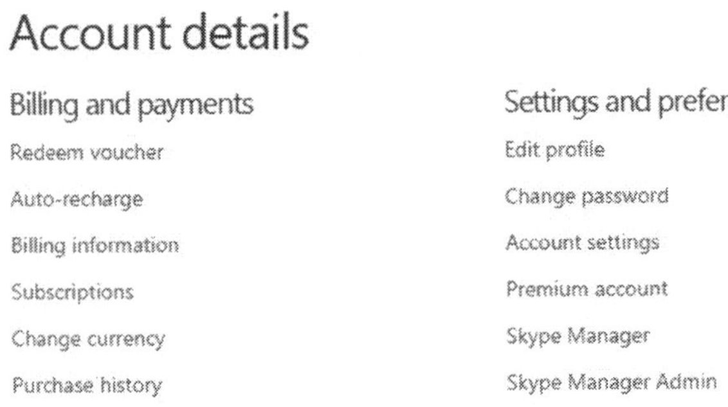

Account details

Billing and payments

Redeem voucher

Auto-recharge

Billing information

Subscriptions

Change currency

Purchase history

Settings and preferences

Edit profile

Change password

Account settings

Premium account

Skype Manager

Skype Manager Admin

Figure 9-2. My Account details

These include options to:

- Redeem Skype Gift vouchers
- Set up an auto-recharge to reload Skype Credit
- Review billing information (name, address, credit card, PayPal accounts)
- Manage subscriptions
- Set the currency used for your purchases
- Review purchase history
- View and edit your Skype profile

- Change your password

- Manage Account settings: links to Microsoft and Facebook account; notifications

- Access a Skype Manager account (see below for more details)

For additional security Skype has established a few policies when dealing with your account:

- An individual credit card may only be associated with one personal Skype account.

- Skype has established monthly purchase limits[1] as one inhibitor to fraud.

- After ten minutes of inactivity, Skype will log you out of your Skype Account screen and ask you to log in again.

From your Skype Account web page you're free to select and purchase the offerings that you require and customize your Settings and preferences; it's basically how you can customize your Skype activity to your individual requirements.

To activate a subscription, click Add subscription on the Manage Account page left sidebar. This brings you to the Rates page where you can select a termination country (see Figure 9-3) where there are a variety of options available. Initially select a termination country. For Canada there are both Pay-As-You-Go option to buy Skype Credit and three subscription options; other countries may include plans with limited minutes. The Details links describe the actual countries covered by a particular subscription. Select an option and proceed to enter payment information via credit card or PayPal to initialize a subscription.

---

[1]https://support.skype.com/en/faq/FA1137/What-are-monthly-purchase-limits

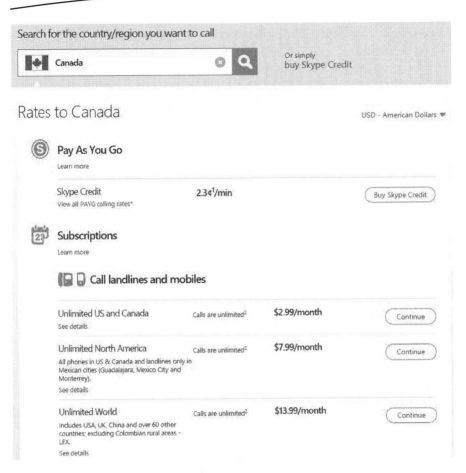

Figure 9-3. Launching a subscription

Let's go on to a few tips that help to ensure you are getting maximum value at minimum overall costs.

Optimizing Your Skype Activities and Associated Costs

It is important to consider the balance between the services you need for your routine Skype activities and the associated costs. Some considerations include:

- Where do you call frequently? Within a single country, continent, or worldwide?

  - Calling Subscription Plans options are broken down along these geographical regions.

  - Payments can be monthly, quarterly (5% discount), or annually (15% discount)

  - Calling plans are based on the call destination country. For example, calling to Canada/U.S. landlines and mobile phones from other countries worldwide are included in a Canada/U.S. calling plan subscription.

- Do you have an Office 365 subscription?

  - If so, you have 60 minutes worldwide per month already available to over 60 countries.

  - Ensure you have linked your Skype account to your Microsoft account via Account settings (see Figure 9-2)

- Are you frequently "roaming" outside your home country?

  - If so, data charges become important. Put your phone in Airplane mode and look for Wi-Fi access points or consider a Truphone World Plan. (See Chapter 6 for more details.)

- Do you call mobile phone numbers in "caller pay" countries, defined in Chapter 8?

  - If so, you will need to have Skype Credit in addition to any Calling Plan Subscriptions.

In the example in Figure 9-1 I have both an Unlimited World subscription and an Office 365 subscription. When it comes time to renew my 12-month Unlimited World subscription I will change to an Unlimited North America (Canada and U.S.) subscription as the Office 365 allowance is sufficient for the number of landline calls I make outside of North America. In practice most of my calls outside North America tend to be Skype-to-Skype calls, whereas in my office, I usually use Skype for calls to landlines and mobile phones within North America. On devices where I have no carrier connection, such as my iPad with Wi-Fi support only, I use Skype over

Wi-Fi when I need to call landlines from the iPad. I also keep in reserve a minimum amount of Skype credit for any calls to mobile phones in caller pays countries.

A few more tips related to managing your Skype Account:

- **Auto-recharge:** for Skype Credit you can set up auto-recharge. In North America when your Skype Credit drops below $3.00 it will do an auto-recharge to the default amount ($10.00 in U.S.; C$14.00 in Canada). This allows you to continue use of your calling activities without interruption while traveling, for instance.

- **Redeem vouchers:** vouchers are supplied by some Skype partners; also Skype gift cards are available. These may be redeemed via the Redeem vouchers option, shown earlier in Figure 9-2.

HOW SKYPE BECAME LESS EXPENSIVE IN 2014

During 2014 Skype made some important changes such that my annual Skype expenses will become significantly reduced in 2014. These include:

- Free Group Video calling along with elimination of Skype Premium (over $100/year); in fact I received a credit for unused time in the form of Skype Credits.

- Office 365 now includes 60 minutes per month of free landline calling to over 60 countries, as well a mobile calling to 8 countries. As a result I am changing my Worldwide Calling Plan subscription (over $100/year) to a U.S./Canada one (less than $40/year) as I still use Skype almost daily for calls to landlines in U.S./Canada from my PC or mobile smartphone.

- At the same time I do ensure there is some Skype Credit available to cover SMS messages and calls to mobile phones in caller pays countries.

Of course, where possible I do make Skype-to-Skype calls due to not only the zero cost but also the excellent voice quality and HD video quality.

Managing Skype in a Business

For business use there are two scenarios for managing Skype activity across the business.

Accounts Managed by Individuals

In this scenario employees at a business usually manage their PC configurations individually. For their Skype implementation they create personal Skype accounts, participate in Group Chats, arrange individual Calling Plan subscriptions (as described in Chapter 7), purchase Skype credit, and take advantage of the various multi-party calling, file sharing and desktop sharing Skype features to enhance their Skype-to-Skype conversations.

Fundamentally this mode involves using Skype's "individual user" features for business communications with no management administration involved.

Accounts Managed by an Administrator

In this scenario, a Skype Administrator is designated to be responsible for Skype Manager, a web-based management tool that lets you centrally manage Skype across a business or organization (or even across your family). A designated Administrator can create and log in to a Skype Manager via the Features ➤ Business menu items at the Skype website. Scroll down to find the link to set up or log in to a Skype Manager account using your Microsoft ID. Login requires using the Administrator's Microsoft account login.

The Skype administrator can manage members' Skype activities via the Skype Manager and implement Skype across Windows PCs via the business version of Skype[2] that can be remotely installed from an administrator's PC. (Mac users can install Skype for Mac on individual PCs; mobile users can install the appropriate Skype application onto their device.) The Skype Manager navigation bar (see Figure 9-4) provides access to a Dashboard, Members, Features, and Reports.

Figure 9-4. Skype Manager

---

[2]http://www.skype.com/intl/en-us/business/download

With Skype Manager the business takes control of employee usage, inbound and outbound calling paths, and subscription costs while having access to call detail records across the business (but still requires call recording utilities for voice and video call conversations).

Figure 9-5 shows the Skype Manager dashboard, including a summary of the manager's own account balance, and key information about the Skype users (members) being managed from this account.

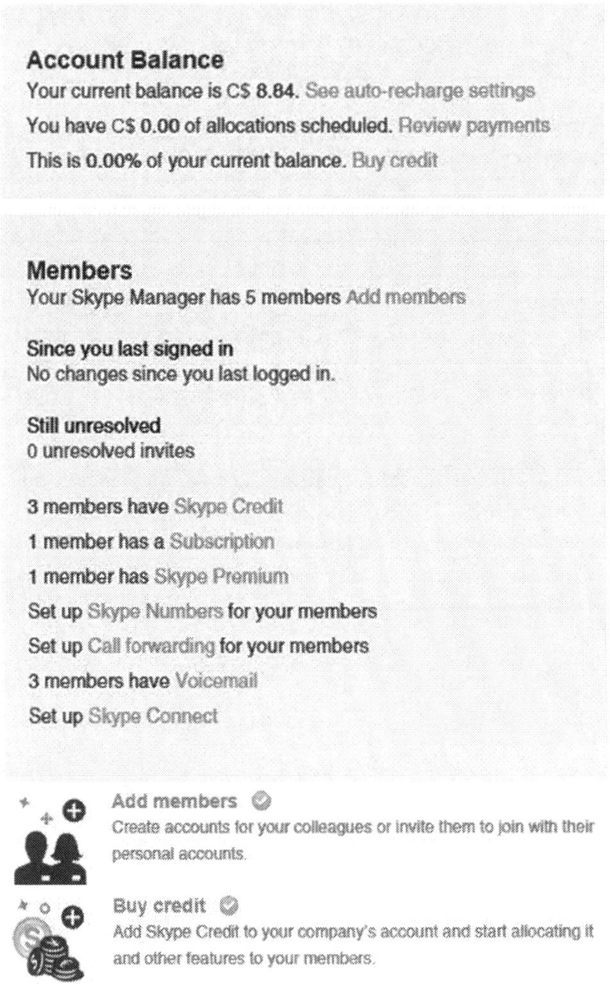

Account Balance

Your current balance is C$ 8.84. See auto-recharge settings

You have C$ 0.00 of allocations scheduled. Review payments

This is 0.00% of your current balance. Buy credit

Members

Your Skype Manager has 5 members Add members

Since you last signed in
No changes since you last logged in.

Still unresolved
0 unresolved invites

3 members have Skype Credit

1 member has a Subscription

1 member has Skype Premium

Set up Skype Numbers for your members

Set up Call forwarding for your members

3 members have Voicemail

Set up Skype Connect

Add members ✓
Create accounts for your colleagues or invite them to join with their personal accounts.

Buy credit ✓
Add Skype Credit to your company's account and start allocating it and other features to your members.

Figure 9-5. Skype Manager Dashboard

The designated administrator uses Skype Manager to:

- Create (and delete) Skype accounts[3] for individual users (employees, contractors, etc.)
  - Often a business will establish a standard Skype ID format, for example, business_name.user_name
- Invite individuals with a personal Skype account to join
- Create Skype Numbers (for Individual Users)
- Set up Calling Plan subscriptions for Individual Users' Skype Accounts
- Purchase Skype Credit on behalf of the business or organization
- Allocate Skype Credit to Users
- Pull unused Skype credit pulled back into the Skype Manager account for reallocation
- Assign which Skype features a User can use (such as file transfer)
- Setup Voice Mail (for individual Users' Business Skype Accounts)
- Monitor Usage through reports
- Create Skype Connect profiles to make outbound Skype calls through an existing SIP-enabled PBX that supports Skype Connect

A major use of Skype Manager is to allocate and manage Skype Credit to members. Navigate to the Features page and select Credit allocations from the sidebar menu (see Figure 9-6). The resulting list shows the current status of Skype credit allocations to each member along with links to Manage Credit and Manage Auto-recharge for each member. The Administrator can also pull back into the manager's pool Skype Credits (especially useful when an employee leaves an organization).

---

[3]http://blogs.skype.com/enterprise/2011/04/sm_what_are_business_accounts.html

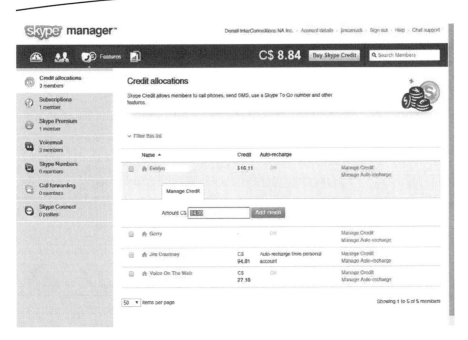

Figure 9-6. Managing Features including Skype Credit

From other options in the sidebar you can also create subscriptions, manage voice mail activity, assign Skype Online Numbers, and manage call forwarding to landlines and mobile phones

▪ Note that Skype Premium is no longer available now that Group Video calling is free.

▪ Skype Connect provides a path for SIP connections to supported third-party PBX systems.

Summary

My Account is the Skype portal to purchase and manage your Skype subscriptions, online numbers, caller ID, call forwarding, and voice messaging. In addition, it provides access to manage billing and payments as well as usage reports. Skype Manager is a web-based portal for administering Skype activity across a business.

Key Points

▨ Skype operates on a pay-in-advance basis, using either Skype Credit or Skype calling plans.

  ▨ With Skype you never receive a phone bill.

▨ Skype calling plans can be optimized for local country, continent, or worldwide calling activity

  ▨ An Office 365 subscription includes 60 minutes of worldwide Skype calling to over 60 countries.

▨ The web-based My Account Skype portal allows users to manage the services and subscriptions associated with an individual account as well as payment and billing options.

  ▨ Businesses can either let employees manage their individual Skype accounts or administer Skype use across the business using Skype Manager.

Chapter 10

Hardware Considerations: PCs, Mobiles, and Peripherals

Perhaps the biggest user experience change in voice calling with Skype is the transition from a legacy desktop or wall phone to the wide range of platforms and devices on which you can make and receive Skype calls: PCs, smartphones, TVs, Blu-ray players, and tablets. Most come with applications that can completely replace the desktop phone yet carry out the functionality of a business desktop phone.

As mentioned previously, Skype requires as an end point a hardware device that incorporates Skype software, whether as an application (PCs, smartphones, tablets) or embedded into an intelligent device's firmware (TVs, Blu-ray players). So the hardware device you use must meet minimum requirements to run Skype software.

In addition consideration must be given to the microphone and speakers, and, for video calls, a webcam–whether embedded or from a third-party vendor. Speakerphones open up additional configurations for participating in voice conversations, especially when multiple participants are gathered in an office or conference room.

Hardware Requirements

While today's PCs tend to have more powerful multi-core processors running at speeds well over 2.0 GHz with multi-GB of RAM memory, there are minimum requirements for using Skype on a Windows PC or Mac (see Table 10-1).

Table 10-1. Minimum Requirements for Using Skype on a PC or Mac

	Windows PC	**Mac**
Skype version	Skype 7.0 for Windows Desktop	Skype 7.0 for Mac
Operating system	Windows XP SP3, Vista, 7, 8.1	Mac OS X 10.9 (Mavericks), 10.10 (Yosemite)
Minimum processor speed (CPU) (voice only)	1.0 GHz	1.0 GHz (Core 2 Duo)
Recommended processor speed (video)	1.8 GHz dual core	2.0 GHz dual core
RAM	512 MB	1 GB
Additional software	DirectX v9.0 or later	Latest version of QuickTime

The evolution of PCs and Macs with dual- and quad-core processors, such as Intel's iCore line, has also contributed to improving the robustness, reliability, and performance of Skype voice and video calls.

For mobile devices the hardware configuration is basically defined with the only option being user accessible memory (16GB, 32GB, 64GB, etc.–either embedded or via an SD card). However, as new devices appear they have faster processors and graphics displays; these allow Skype's developers to modify the user interface, improve the audio and video performance (such as the recent upgrades supporting HD quality video), reduce battery drain (significantly), as well as introduce new features such as video messaging.

Choosing Peripheral Hardware

While all PCs incorporate a microphone and speakers and some notebooks and PC display monitors include a webcam, there are many reasons to consider third-party accessories such as headsets, webcams, and speakerphones:

- To take full advantage of Skype's proprietary voice technology that can deliver crystal-clear audio on Skype-to-Skype calls between PCs, iPhone, Android, iPad, BlackBerry 10, Windows Phone, TVs, and Blu-ray players

- To take full advantage of Skype's proprietary video technology that can deliver High Quality (VGA) or HD (720p or 1080p) Video on Skype-to-Skype calls at relatively low upload speeds

- To provide privacy in open office and other noisy background environments

- To allow you to move away from your PC during a voice call (using a wireless headset)

- To ensure optimal voice quality (microphone, speakers)

To establish benchmarks for peripheral performance Skype developed, over its first eight or nine years, a Skype-certified hardware program that assisted in ensuring that users can take full advantage of these features. However, over this period PC vendors introduced embedded webcams supporting HD video and higher performance audio hardware, while peripheral vendors also introduced higher performance webcams, microphones, headsets, and speakerphones whose specifications have become standard across several vendors.

As a result the market for hardware peripherals took a severe decline and the need for an ongoing certification program evaporated. What at one time produced excitement over its innovation has now evolved into industry standard performance across the peripherals market.

While Skype certification addressed technical and user experience issues, it did not address features on a product such as whether a webcam includes a microphone or a headset that includes a volume control. Those are product marketing decisions of the individual peripheral hardware vendors.

What follows provides guidelines and considerations to be taken into account when purchasing these peripherals in today's market.

Where do you find these peripherals? The former Skype Shop is migrating into the Microsoft Store; accessories are available on the Microsoft U.S. Store and will become available in other countries over time. Skype has also designated Chat and Vision[1] as a Skype Global Merchant Partner (see Figure 10-1). Third-party vendors, such as Logitech, ClearOne, Creative Labs, and Plantronics include a website store and/or make them available via Amazon and other e-commerce vendors. Of course many items can also be purchased in electronics retail stores.

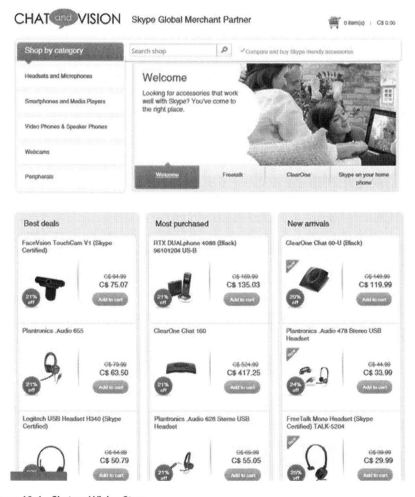

Figure 10-1. Chat and Vision Store

---

[1]https://ca.chatandvision.com/skype_shop

When buying from a third-party store or website, you will need to be more careful to select hardware with the right specifications for Skype. The Microsoft and Chat and Vision Stores are the safest way to ensure you get hardware that will work well with Skype (see Figure 10-2).

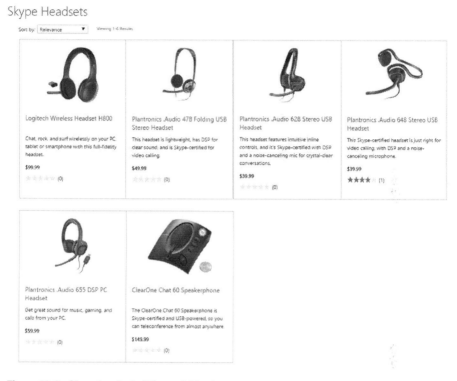

Figure 10-2. Skype headsets (Microsoft Store)

The choice of hardware available can be bewildering. Let's look at some types of hardware starting with the most common Skype accessory: headsets.

Headsets

It's possible to make a Skype call using the built-in speakers and microphone on devices such as laptops and tablets, but to get the best experience, sound quality, echo cancellation, and privacy, a headset is a good investment.

Headsets come in three general styles: supra-aural, circumaural, and in-ear. Supra-aural headsets have smaller, lighter earpads that rest directly on the ear. Circumaural headsets completely cover and surround the ear, resting on the side of the head. In-ear headsets have small ear buds that sit inside the ear, and a microphone built in to the wire. Which kind of headset you prefer will partly come down to personal preference, but some examples of their typical characteristics are:

- Supra-aural headsets are compact and lightweight, but don't block out or contain noise as much as the other two designs.

- Some people find supra-aural and/or in-ear headsets uncomfortable to wear over long periods because they press or sit directly on or in the ears. If you're one of these people, you might find a circumaural headset more comfortable, but be aware that they can also be quite heavy.

- In-ear headsets are small, light, and easy to transport, but the microphone placement might not be ideal for longer or hands-free calling, especially in a noisy environment.

When looking at headsets, some questions to ask yourself might be

- Do I already have a preference for a particular form factor: in-ear, on-ear, or over-ear?

- Will I need to use the headset for long periods?

  - Is the padding comfortable?

  - Is it heavy/light?

  - Is it the right size or fit for me (e.g., right size of ear bud; ear pads not pressing too hard on the ears)?

- Will I be working in a noisy environment?

- Is the microphone placement right for me?

- Will I need to transport it (size/robust design)?

- Is freedom to move around during a call required?

  - Should it be a wireless headset?

- Does the headset support stereo audio?

- Do I want to connect to a PC via a wireless Bluetooth connection, a physical USB port, or 3.5 mm stereo mini-jack?

▓ Do I also want to use the headset with a smartphone, such as an iPhone or BlackBerry, or a media player, such as an iPod, which use either a 3.5mm headset jack or wireless Bluetooth connection?

Some headsets may have multiple connections, for example:

▓ The Logitech H800 wireless headset has options for Bluetooth or a USB wireless adapter.

▓ The Freetalk Everyman, available online from Chat and Vision, includes both a USB adapter and, for listening to your media player or smartphone/tablet, a 3.5 mm stereo headphone jack. It also includes an audio chip that bypasses the audio chip on a PC to assure capturing the full crystal-clear audio available using Skype.

Webcams for PCs

Many PC monitors and most notebook PCs now incorporate a webcam that meets minimum standards for at least High Quality Video and often for HD Video. Skype video calling will also work with most third-party webcams that are supported by Windows or Mac OS X. These usually deliver an acceptable quality video call for personal and business calling.

But how do you get the best quality video?

As its video quality evolved toward supporting HD video resolutions Skype worked with some webcam vendors to develop webcams that could deliver Skype's High Quality Video or HD Video while dealing with the network connection issues and frame rates (frames-per-second) that are required to deliver a video stream that is similar to HD television quality. The key for these webcams was not simply resolution, but also delivering video at the frame rate (frames-per-second or fps) required for a non-flickering or non-pixelating video stream while not impacting Skype's superwideband audio. Today, whether embedded or a peripheral, most webcams support at least High Quality Video (VGA: 640x480). Figure 10-3 shows screenshots of both high-quality and HD video. Although you probably can't see the difference in resolution in the figure, you can see that HD video enables you to use more of your screen real estate. High Quality offers a 4:3 aspect ratio while HD video has a wider 16:9 aspect ratio. This is similar to the difference in ratios between conventional and HD TVs.

High Quality Video
VGA (640 x 480) @ 30 fps

HD Video
720p (1280 x 720) @ 22fps

Figure 10-3. Skype video resolutions

Webcam considerations include:

- What resolution do I want/need?

    - VGA (640 × 480) resolution is the minimum requirement for a realistic video image.

    - HD's 720p (1280 × 720) or 1080p (1920 × 1080) resolution deliver an image that approaches telepresence quality[2], especially when viewing in Full Screen mode on a 20" to 27" monitor.

- What is the video viewing range to be supported? 1.5 meters works for personal video and up to 5 meters for a small to medium size conference room or the family room.

- Can it auto-focus? For example, could it show a business card clearly when brought close to the webcam?

- Does it have a face following feature?

[2]http://www.disruptivetelephony.com/2012/03/skypes-hd-video-quality-is-amazing.html

- Is a microphone or microphone array necessary or desirable?

  - Some webcams include built-in microphones, but a longer-range conference webcam would need to be used in conjunction with a closer-range microphone or microphone array.

- How well does the webcam adapt to low-light conditions?

- Does the webcam include support software for video recording, managing the webcam settings, downloading video to YouTube?

- Is the webcam to be used with a Skype-enabled TV or Blu-ray player?

Figure 10-4 shows some of the webcams available via the Microsoft store. Webcams that support both High Quality Video and HD Video on a Windows PC with a dual core 2.0 GHz processor include:

- Logitech C920 HD Pro Webcam[3] (Windows only)

- Logitech C615[4]/C/525/C310[5]/C270

- faceVsion Touchcam V1 (720p with H.264 processor)

---

[3]http://voiceontheweb.biz/skype-world/skype-ecosystem/skype-partner-solutions/logitech-c920-webcam-superior-skype-video-calling/
[4]http://www.logitech.com/en-us/webcam-communications/webcams/devices/hd-webcam-c615
[5]http://www.logitech.com/en-us/webcam-communications/webcams/devices/7076

Skype Webcams

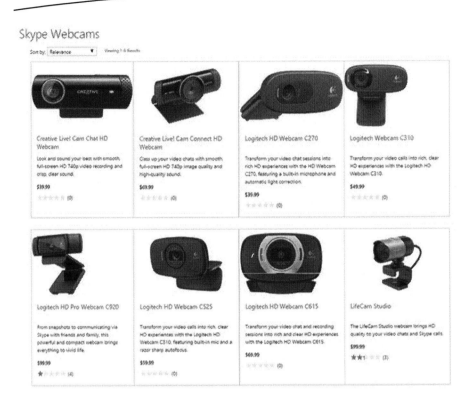

Figure 10-4. Skype webcams (Microsoft Store)

The Logitech C920 HD Video webcams incorporate an embedded H.264 processor to reduce the video image processing load on the PC's primary CPU and the amount of data transmitted over the Internet. These webcams can send/receive 30 frames per second (fps) for High Quality Video and 22 fps for HD video; Logitech HD webcams support 30 fps for HD video.

Sending video to your contacts is an upload activity from your PC or TV. Whereas High Quality Video requires a minimum 512 Kbps upload speed for the Internet connection, HD Video webcams require a minimum 1.0 to 1.2 Mbps upload speed for 720p video or 2.0 Mbps for 1080p. A webcam will send High Quality Video if there is insufficient upload speed for HD Video.

> **Note**   A couple of comments about the Logitech C920 (Windows only): in tests with the Logitech C920 webcam it uniquely supports:
>
> - 720p video at up to 30 fps; requires 1.0 Mbps upload speed
> - 1080p video; requires 2.0 Mbps upload speed
>
> Other brands supplying webcams include Creative Labs Live! and Lifecam Studio.

Webcams for TV

In early 2010, with the emergence of smart TVs that had an Internet connection, Skype started appearing embedded into Samsung, Sony, LG, and other vendors' high-end TVs. By 2014 Smart TV with the inclusion of Skype has become a standard feature on all but the lowest-end HDTV sets from these brands.

Today Skype is available on smart HDTV sets from LG, Panasonic, Philips, Samsung, Sharp, Sony, Toshiba, and Vizio. Check with the individual vendors to see which models include at least a smart TV feature. It is also available on Blu-ray players from Panasonic, Philips, and Sony.

When investigating TVs with embedded Skype check for the following:

- Is the webcam embedded in the TV set or do you need to purchase a compatible webcam designed to work with that particular model?

- If you need to buy a webcam, does it support a two- or four-microphone array for picking up audio across a small conference room or family room? Webcams used with Skype for TV must be able to pick up multiple voices as far as 4 to 6 meters (15 to 20 feet) away from the webcam, so these webcams include 2 or 4 microphones with noise cancelling. Skype for TV firmware has been optimized to ensure audio quality integrity in such a scenario.

> **Note**   Skype for TV can only be used for one-to-one Skype calls; it cannot be used as a participant on a multi-party voice or video call. To view a multi-party call on a TV display requires use of Skype on a PC with an appropriate setup to use the TV display as a PC monitor.

All webcams include a wide-angle lens to capture everyone in the room within the video image.

An All-In-One Solution for HDTV Sets

If you have a flat panel HDTV set with an HDMI connection, one option you might want to consider is a telyHD, which brings Skype for TV to any HDTV set (see Figure 10-5). This is an all-in-one hardware and software (Android-based) solution made by Tely Labs.

Figure 10-5. Skype on TelyHD

The TelyHD:

- Embeds a wide-angle HD webcam supporting 720p resolution at 30 frames per second (fps), with a privacy shutter

- Includes four noise cancelling microphones that take advantage of Skype's audio processing technology

- Requires an HDTV set with an HDMI input

- Incorporates a remote control for managing the Skype calling experience from across the room

- Makes calls to Skype contacts on PCs, smartphones, and tablets, Skype for TV and other telyHDs

- Includes an onboard H.264 processor to reduce the video codec processing load on the main processor

- Connects to the Internet via either Wi-Fi or an Ethernet cable

- Includes a USB port for a wired/wireless keyboard and/ or USB memory stick for photo sharing

telyHD Base Edition can be upgraded to telyHD Pro via a software upgrade. This is a full business teleconferencing system providing interoperability across multiple video conferencing offerings.

Speakerphones and Microphones

While using the native PC's audio hardware or headsets certainly meets the basic requirements for participating in a voice call, situations will arise where it is preferable to:

- Have several people participate on the call via a shared audio device

- Use Skype in a family room, office, or conference room

- Not be seen wearing a microphone during a video call or video call recording

- Use a high-quality microphone, especially when recording

For these situations a speakerphone addresses these requirements. The major consideration for a speakerphone decision is whether you want a short-range personal speakerphone or a long- range speakerphone configuration, such as the length of a conference room table.

Other considerations include:

- Ability to fit readily into a briefcase (personal speakerphones)

- Power source, a USB connection or independent power supply

- Echo cancellation

One vendor of high-quality speakerphones is ClearOne with their ChatAttach series (see Figure 10-6).

Figure 10-6. *ClearOne Chat 160*

Microphones come in many forms, such as those included with headsets and free standing mics. They usually provide sufficient quality for normal conversations. Some microphones associated with capturing conversation in a meeting room may deal with issues such as echo cancellation; others, such as the Yeti Blue, are recognized for their broadcast quality, appropriate for use in, say, podcasts.

Summary

With Skype, the end point for placing and receiving calls becomes intelligent hardware, whether PCs, smartphones, tablets or TVs and DVD players. Skype's technology, along with its options for video, file sharing, echo cancellation and more, is more advanced than traditional phone technology and comes with certain minimum hardware requirements. In addition to this, you will often need or want supporting hardware such as a headset, webcam or conferencing solution. When choosing hardware to use with Skype, you need to decide what factors matter to you, whether it's price, comfort, convenience, or audio and video quality.

Key Points

▓ The evolution of duo- and quad-core processors has been a major factor that has contributed to more reliable, robust, and sustainable Skype conversations.

▓ Whether embedded into the hardware or acquired as third-party peripherals, high-performance webcams, headsets, and microphones are required to achieve superwideband audio and HD video Skype calling.

▓ Some webcams include built-in microphones or microphone arrays.

▓ Most TV sets are now "smart," with Internet connectivity built in and the ability to run Skype for TV. Some smart TVs come with the necessary hardware (webcam, microphone array) built in, while others require you to buy your own.

▓ The telyHD Basic Edition is one way to bring Skype voice and video calling to any HDTV equipped with an HDMI connection, and can be upgraded to telyHD Pro for use as a full business teleconferencing system.

Building Geographically Dispersed Teams Over Skype

One key to a profitable and effective business is building team rapport across employees. This is accomplished more readily when everyone is in one location. However, with the rise of geographically dispersed business teams, the ability to easily converse spontaneously across continents and oceans at little or no cost becomes an essential ingredient for success.

As a result Skype has become a key to not only building business teams that comprise the best resources available worldwide but also to generating revenues internationally with minimum overhead. While Skype helps minimize travel expenses, it also keeps in contact with those team members who do have to travel.

Skype and Collaboration: Building Teams and Communities

Skype supports multi-party (or Group) Chat, Voice, and Video conversations that are available free to all Skype users. This includes Group Video calling. Skype supports both the collaboration activities of business teams and special interest groups working around the world, as well as *ad hoc* consumer conversations, such as a family conference call.

Personally I have participated in very productive multi-party voice and video calls with participants in North America, Europe, South Africa, and Hong Kong; the main challenge is finding a time convenient for all parties across time zones spanning up to 15 hours. I have also participated in multiple Group chats, some of which have been running (and archived) since May 2007.

While there are other voice and video conferencing options they tend to be managed services, whereas Skype is more ad hoc, supporting both asynchronous (text) and real time (text, voice, and video) conversations. Skype has unique features when conferencing such as:

- All conversation text-based information (chat messages, file transfers, URL's, call detail records, etc.) is archived and searchable.

    - Voice and video recordings require third-party applications such as Pamela on Windows PC's and Call Recorder for Mac

- It's available on all platforms: participants in a group conversation can be on PCs, iOS, Android devices, BlackBerry 10, and Windows Phones.

- All activity is buffered such that:

    - It is transcribed across the various devices the account is logged into.

    - Messages sent to a user while offline appear when the user goes back online.

Creating a Group

Creating a Group involves starting with a selected contact and clicking on the ⊛ icon (see Figure 11-1) in the conversation pane's header. This results in a drop-down list of all your (Skype) Contacts. Here you can search for and check all those you want to add and then click the Add to Group button. Figure 11-1 shows adding a contact to a group already containing seven people. The same process applies even when adding the first person to a group.

Figure 11-1. Building a group

After you add a contact to a group the new participant receives a chat notification (see Figure 11-2).

Jim Courtney added **Voice On The Web**

8:37 AM

Figure 11-2. Group participation notification

The new contact may see earlier messages in the Group Chat along with all new messages going forward. If the participant wants to leave the Group, right-click the Group name in the Contacts pane and select Leave Conversation or select "Conversation | Leave Conversation" from the main drop-down menu.

A topic for the group can be set using the /topic [text] command (no square brackets). Ensure the topic briefly, but adequately describes the purpose of the group. The creator of the group assumes the ADMIN role, while other participants are USERs unless others are assigned an ADMIN or MASTER role using the /setrole command shown in Figure 11-3.

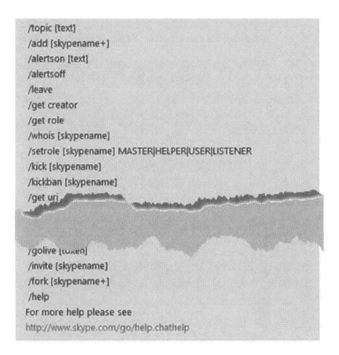

```
/topic [text]
/add [skypename+]
/alertson [text]
/alertsoff
/leave
/get creator
/get role
/whois [skypename]
/setrole [skypename] MASTER|HELPER|USER|LISTENER
/kick [skypename]
/kickban [skypename]
/get uri




/golive [token]
/invite [skypename]
/fork [skypename+]
/help
For more help please see
http://www.skype.com/go/help.chathelp
```

Figure 11-3. Group Chat administration options

Alternatively, a group can be created using "Contacts | Create New Group" from the Skype client main menu. Once again, click the ⊕ icon and proceed as described previously.

For management and administration of various parameters governing the chat session, type /help and a list of the various setting options appears in the chat window (see Figure 11-3). At the end of the list is a link to obtain more details about each option.

Group Chat: Skype as a Virtual Water Fountain

Let's start with the most used collaboration tool: Group Chat. A Group Chat (see Figure 11-4):

- can include up to 300 participants,
- is persistent over time and
- acts as a virtual worldwide water cooler.

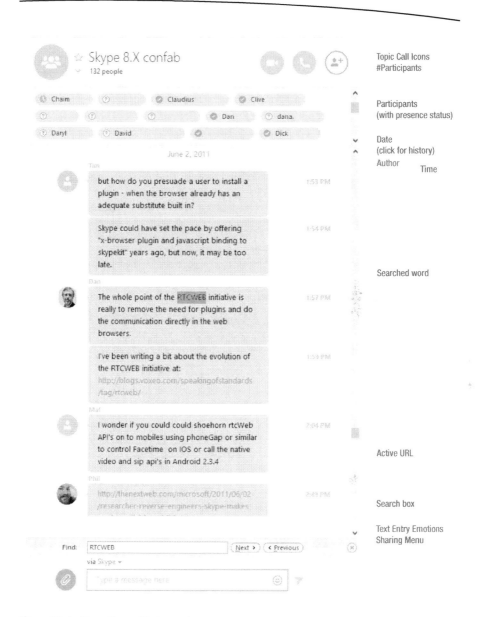

Figure 11-4. Skype Group Chat overview

Keep in mind that Group Chats should be contributing to not only the business operations but also the internal culture and team building within the business. Best practices guidelines should be established to reinforce the need to focus on the business team's goals, while keeping the conversation constructive, respecting the views of other ethically, and avoiding "trash talk."

One person creates a Group Chat and adds the initial participants as outlined in the previous section; others can be added as an Admin (Moderator) or Speaker (Participant) via the /setrole command. As with chat sessions with individual contacts, Group Chat contents are stored on your local PC and are searchable; however, a warning: following a very active greater than 50 participant Group Chat over a long period of time can consume considerable storage on your PC.

In practice, Group Chats can be somewhat ad hoc in that often a session may remain quiet for a few days and then go very active when a hot topic arises.

When used in business or as a virtual community forum, it is wise to adopt a specific operational role for a Group Chat, usually defined through the Topic setting (/topic) described earlier in this chapter. Assigning a topic also helps to enforce a business discipline such that chat activity stays focused on its primary topic and does not wander into conversations irrelevant to the primary agenda for the Group Chat.

Chat conversation messages may comprise a mix of those that require immediate action and those that are involved simply to discuss a topic of interest that provides dialogue and background for future activities or projects. In a business environment, there should be an inherent discipline not only to keep the conversation on topic but also to ensure participants have an implicit understanding of what type of message requires an immediate action.

Files and photos can be transferred only to Group participants who are also the sending participant's accepted Contacts. Starting with Skype 7.0 for Windows Desktop and Mac, the transferred file is represented by either a thumbnail of an image (see Figure 11-5) or a document file image related to the relevant application (see Figure 11-6). Click the image to either view the photo or download the document into the relevant application itself.

Figure 11-5. File transfer image for a photo or image file

Figure 11-6. File transfer image for a document file

When you send a file transfer to a group you can actually see who has downloaded the file. If all have accepted or the transfer is cancelled after a few have accepted you can click on the "sent to n people" link to see who has accepted (see Figure 11-7).

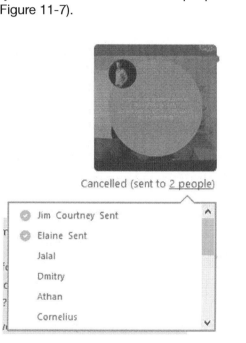

Figure 11-7. Group File Transfer Acceptance List

A business operation will often have multiple Group Chats built around business operations teams and/or designated projects.

Group Chats can be escalated to a multi-party Voice call with up to 25 participants and a Group Video call with up to 10 participants simply by clicking the appropriate icon in the Group Chat header.

Group Chats can be recalled back to their beginning. Click on a "date" at the top of the conversation pane and you can select how far back you want to view or scroll (see Figure 11-8).

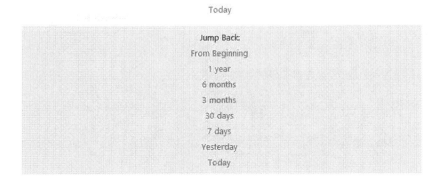

Figure 11-8. Recalling archived conversations

Using Ctrl-F (Windows)/Command-F (Mac) you can search for a word or phrase back through the entire archived period. In Figure 11-4 a search was done for the acronym RTCWEB and searched messages entered over three years ago.

Multi-Party Voice Calls: Travel-Free Conferencing

Multi-party Voice calls are hosted on the originator's PC and can support up to 25 participants. Beyond adding or removing participants to/from the call, the host has little control over the call's flow. All parties are visible, via their avatar, in the Skype conversation/chat pane. One very helpful feature is a blue "halo" appearing around the avatar of the person who is currently speaking.

If a host's PC is not powerful enough to support the call or has a weak Internet connection, another participant with a more powerful PC or more robust Internet connection can easily become the host and reconnect the call. Simply select the previously created Group from the Contact pane and click on the "Phone" icon in the Group conversation pane header. Should there be more than 25 participants in the Group, you will be asked to select those participants whom you want to include on the call.

Skype's multi-party calling is great for ad hoc and intra-company multi-party calls. However, for robust managed conference calls hosted on a server, you must register for and deploy third-party offerings such as Microsoft Lync, GoToMeeting, Uberconference, or FreeConference. These offerings provide moderator features, such as participant muting and hand raising. They often will include a chat session and can at least share documents. Most importantly these offerings can support several hundred or even thousands of participants, most of whom would be in a "listener" mode.

Whereas five to ten party conference calls on the legacy phone network could quickly run up a significant bill, Skype's multi-party Voice calls are either totally free if all parties are on Skype or invoke landline/mobile calling charges only for each of those participants on a landline or mobile phone.

> **Note**   Skype recently released Skype 5.4 for iPhone, which supports hosting a Group Voice call with up to four participants. Skype expects to release other mobile versions with a similar feature, provided the underlying hardware (processor, RAM) can handle the hosting.

WHY MIGHT YOU CHOOSE A MANAGED COLLABORATION SERVICE OVER SKYPE?

Skype's free multi-party services involve hosting the session on a Skype user's PC. For this reason, Skype on smartphones (iPhone Android, BlackBerry 10, or Windows Phone), only supports participation, but not hosting on a Skype multi-party call. Also sessions hosted on a user's PC may be limited due to other programs running on the PC, bandwidth of the Internet connection, or even the processor speed–a minimum 2GHz dual-core processor is recommended.

But, other than to add or remove participants to/from a call, the host has little control over the flow of the call.

Third-party managed services, on the other hand, allow a host or moderator to manage other aspects of the call, such as:

- Muting of participants and selecting which participants can speak

- Hand raising to allow a participant to indicate an interest in speaking

- Invitations can be sent out prior to the call along with information on how to call in

- Call-in via Skype or local phone numbers (worldwide in some services)

- Presentation mode: Support for 100s or even 1000s of participants

- Chat sessions seen by all participants on the call

- Document sharing, desktop sharing, and/or file management features are common options

- Host robustness and participant scalability via a robust, scalable, managed server

- Meeting rooms that are persistently available with supporting content

- Call recording and archiving for later access

Group Video Calling: Togetherness Across Continents and Oceans

While Group Chat and Voice offer opportunities to build team rapport, a Group Video session provides the ability to hold virtual conference room meetings with participants located anywhere at multiple locations worldwide. It delivers opportunities to graphically reinforce an issue or offering through a visual demonstration, perform screen sharing for slide presentations and document reviews, as well as add visual emotion to a virtual conference room meeting through facial expressions and arm waving gestures.

Skype initially launched Group Video calling requiring a Skype Premium subscription; however, over the summer of 2014 it became a free offering. Including the host, a Skype Group Video call can support up to ten participants. Skype Group Video supports participation by Skype contacts at no cost. However, it also can include "voice only" participants added via their landline or mobile number; this feature does require that the host has either Skype credit or a Skype Calling Plan to landlines and mobile.

As with Group Voice calls, Group Video calls can only be hosted on Windows PCs and Macs, yet participants can join the call on mobile devices. If it's a hybrid meeting where several participants are in a headquarters office or conference room and others participate remotely, it's recommended to use a large display screen in the physical office/conference room with microphones or speakerphones equipped to pick up audio from anyone in the room (more details in Chapter 10).

When a Skype Group Video call is launched, a dark background comes down in your conversation pane and shows either video images of the other participants or their Skype profile avatar. Generally if a user either has no webcam or a poor Internet connection that won't support video, he or she can still participate on a call as a voice participant where he or she appears as a Skype profile avatar.

In Figure 11-9, the call involves participants in Canada and the U.S. but readily can incorporate participants worldwide. However, user "Voice On The Web" did not have a webcam; this represents a voice-only participant.

Figure 11-9. *Group Video call screen*

Note that, during the call, the host can click on the Group Chat icon (lower right) to lift the blind sufficiently to see an accompanying text chat pane. If the Skype client window is wide enough, the chat session appears as right sidebar (Figure 11-10); otherwise it appears below the Call Screen. All participants can contribute to and view the chat dialogue.

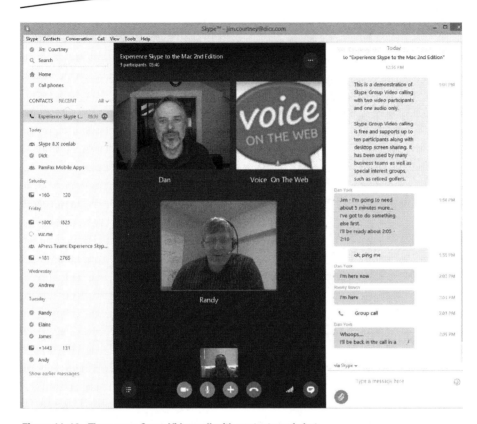

Figure 11-10. Three pane Group Video call with contacts and chat

During the call one user can also share a desktop screen or individual windows within the desktop.

Clicking the arrow icon in the top left of the call screen removes the Contacts pane.

Figure 11-11. Group Video call screen header

The participants' images will move around the screen as the speakers change as determined by Skype's embedded algorithms. Figure 11-12 is an example in which the speaker at the moment appears as a much larger video image.

Figure 11-12. Group Video call- speaker appears in larger image

Clicking the Full Screen option on the three-dot menu in the upper right opens up a Full Screen view (Figure 11-13). This is where the images are approaching telepresence.

Figure 11-13. Group Video call full screen

If you move to another application on the desktop, the call continues and the Call Monitor window appears showing whoever is talking at the time (see Figure 11-14).

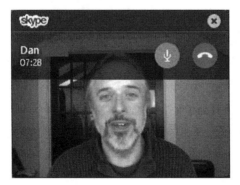

Figure 11-14. Group Video call monitor window

As with Skype multi-party Voice calls, calls are hosted on the host's local PC and do not offer full conference call managed hosting features.

Group Video calls support only VGA resolution (640 × 480). This is more of a pragmatic "available screen real estate" issue rather than a technical limitation when viewing multiple video images within a display's overall resolution.

Summary

Skype's Group conversation features are especially useful for creating an ad hoc virtual office environment across a geographically disbursed business. Water fountain chat sessions keep colleagues up to date on activity within the business, while providing a forum for informal and formal discussion of designated topics.

Skype's Group conversation features offer very low cost communications services for building a small business or startup that needs to focus on cost control, even for working with suppliers and providing customer service. On the other hand, businesses of any size may want to deploy Skype for its face-to-face high quality video and/or crystal clear voice quality on Skype-to-Skype calls.

Key Points

▓ It's easy to create a contact group on Skype by going to an existing contact or conversation and clicking on the ⊕ icon to add participants. You can name a group by team or topic to make it easy to find.

▓ Skype Group Chat provides an informal environment for building virtual water fountain discussions across a worldwide business ecosystem.

▓ Skype Group Voice calling provides an easily configured service for voice conference calls with fewer than 25 active participants.

▓ Skype Group Video becomes a virtual conference room for geographically dispersed businesses.

Chapter 12

Skype on Office 365, Outlook.com and Lync

When Microsoft acquired Skype they were not only looking at improving the Skype user experience on PCs and mobile devices but also realized there were opportunities to enable Skype-enriched communications within other Microsoft platforms such as Office Online, incorporating Outlook. com (formerly Hotmail), Office, and Lync. At the same time Microsoft was rebuilding Skype's back end infrastructure to facilitate the completion of these integrations.

Shortly after the Microsoft acquisition of Skype, Microsoft migrated Hotmail to Outlook.com, a more fully featured web-based communications service, incorporating email, Skype, and some social networking. The embedding of Skype access has evolved to the point where an Outlook.com website becomes a more unified web-based communications platform that includes both email and Skype on a single "web page" without the need to use a dedicated Skype client. In turn, Outlook.com has been incorporated into Microsoft's evolving Office Online applications, several of which now include, or will soon include, Skype integration.

Enabling Skype's communications infrastructure within an online application allows the user the flexibility to access the various online applications from any web browser without the need to use a Skype client. This is particularly useful when using third-party PCs in, say, public locations such as libraries and airport lounges. It also facilitates real time collaboration when preparing Word documents and PowerPoint presentations while away from a user's primary desktop PC or laptop.

Skype on Outlook.com

To set up Outlook.com you need to have (or open) a Microsoft account and to have linked your Skype account with your Microsoft account (via the Skype Account profile, see Chapter 9). In a web browser go to Outlook. com where you will be asked to log in to your Microsoft account, click the Messaging (speech bubble) icon to the left of your account name and a screen similar to the one in Figure 12-1 appears.

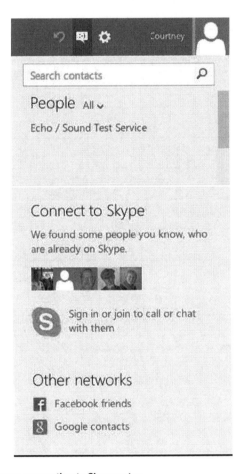

Figure 12-1. Outlook.com connection to Skype setup

Sign in to your Skype account; at some point you will be asked to install a Skype plug-in for your browser. Once you've completed setup, you should see a screen similar to the one shown in Figure 12-2.

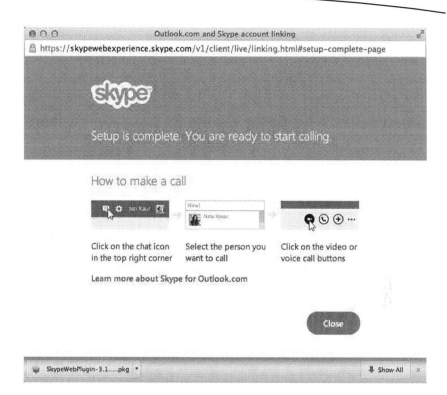

Figure 12-2. Outlook.com completed setup

Either complementary to or, instead of, an Outlook.com email address you can set up Outlook.com to pick up email from other email addresses via POP. To access Skype from the main Outlook.com screen, click the Messenger or chat icon at the right end of the blue navigation bar across the top of the screen. Initially Skype replaces the ads on the right and opens a Recent sidebar (see Figure 12-3). A vertical green bar on the left of an avatar indicates presence status as available for that contact.

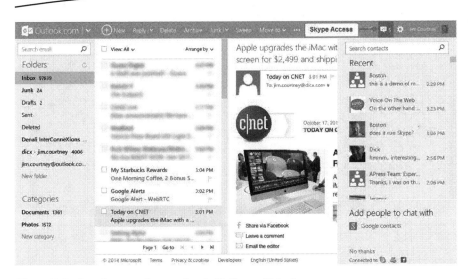

Figure 12-3. Outook.com web page view (with Skype sidebar)

When you click on a Skype contact in the Recent sidebar you can enter text to chat with them and/or launch a voice or video call, or add another person to the conversation, via the appropriate icons (see Figure 12-4). If you want to reach a contact who is not in the Recent chat sidebar, search for the contact in the Search contacts box shown at the top of the sidebar.

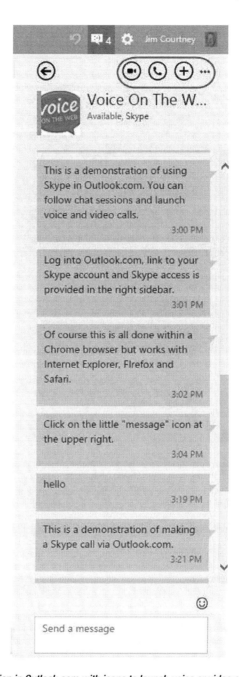

Figure 12-4. Chat session in Outlook.com with icons to launch voice or video call, or add another party

Important to recognize is that Outlook.com is the first component of the evolving Office Online offering (see Figure 12-5).

Figure 12-5. Office Online applications

Skype access is always provided via the same chat icon and right-hand sidebar within People, Calendar, and OneDrive. In addition to Skype conversations, People also provides links to send an email, a Tweet, or a Facebook message, as well as make an entry on the contact's Facebook wall (see Figure 12-6). At the time of writing Skype had announced that Word Online and PowerPoint Online will also incorporate Skype in a similar manner during document collaboration sessions.

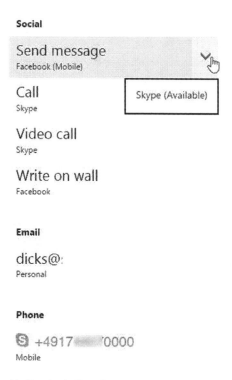

Social

Send message
Facebook (Mobile)

Skype (Available)

Call
Skype

Video call
Skype

Write on wall
Facebook

Email

dicks@:
Personal

Phone

+4917███'0000
Mobile

Figure 12-6. Contact Card in People via Outook.com

When you make a call from an Office Online module, a new frameless window appears with the familiar Skype call background, call management bar and the ability to open the chat discussion as a sidebar (see Figure 12-7). However, as Office Online modules are web-based there is no chat history shown and chat messages are not buffered. If the account is also open in a Skype client on a PC, any chat discussion during the call from an Office Online module is transcribed into the PC client's conversation pane as well as the Office Online module's Skype sidebar. As with other chat messages, when not online in a PC Skype client the message is buffered, ready to appear the next time a PC Skype client is logged in. It also is archived on the PC for later recall.

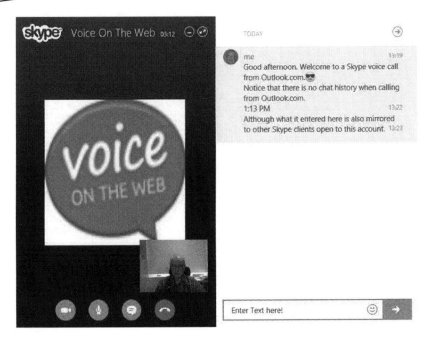

Figure 12-7. Voice Call Screen and Chat using Outlook.com

Outlook.com provides a convenient way to check email and Skype activity via a web browser, especially when using a "foreign" PC that, say, does not have a Skype client readily available. It also provides convenient access to other Office Online modules from any PC- or Mac-based web browser.

> **Note**   Windows Live Messenger migrated to Skype Instant Messaging. When Microsoft acquired Skype they had two real-time communications offerings that duplicated most of the functionality. As a result, all Windows Live Messenger accounts were migrated to Skype accounts, providing a richer feature set that also takes full advantage of Skype's unique voice and video technology.

Skype and Outlook

You can also launch Skype chat, voice, and video conversations from Outlook 2010 and 2013. When viewing an Outlook email message, scroll your mouse over the sender's (or recipient's) name and a box appears with several options (see Figure 12-8).

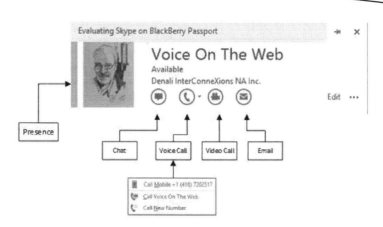

Figure 12-8. Outlook Message header with Skype and email links

Clicking Edit (or a down arrow) at the lower right brings up the full contact card (see Figure 12-9).

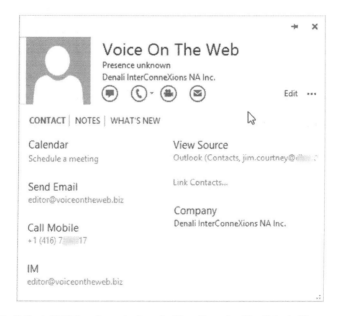

Figure 12-9. Outlook 2013 People contact card with outbound calling link via Skype

In this case clicking the appropriate icon launches a chat session, voice, or video call in the native Skype for Windows Desktop client. Clicking the Email icon opens up a new Outlook message window.

In summary, Outlook provides a convenient way to launch Skype conversations in the Skype for Windows Desktop client when working with email messages, whether sent or received. (Note that it does not launch calls using Skype for Windows Modern).

Microsoft Lync

Microsoft Lync was initially developed as an enterprise-grade unified communications platform providing robust, secure communications across larger enterprises. Lync clients are available across many platforms, including Windows, Mac, iOS, Android, and Windows Phone. Lync provides a consistent, single-client experience for presence, instant messaging, voice, HD video, and also online meeting features.

Lync users can connect to anyone on Skype, extending its instant messaging, presence sharing, and voice calling to the hundreds of millions of Skype users worldwide. In December 2014, Microsoft introduced video calling between Lync and Skype users.

Lync users add Skype contacts by typing their Skype users' Microsoft account names into Lync's Add Skype Contact window (available through 'Add a contact not in my organization'). Skype users can likewise add Lync contacts by typing users' email addresses into the search bar within Skype and clicking Add Contact. This makes it possible to contact a wider network of people through Skype.

Lync was initially targeted to larger businesses with associated Lync server resource requirements. This comes with higher costs, recovered through its enterprise features such as supporting online meetings with hundreds of participants. For the purposes of this book, only the Skype–Lync integration is mentioned; for additional information follow up with Microsoft's Lync website.

However, Lync requires a premise-based or hosted server managed by an enterprise's IT management. Recently Microsoft has begun offering Lync Online as a standalone service within Office 365 where Microsoft provides the required hosting. This allows smaller businesses to take advantage of the Lync feature set at a low monthly per seat cost.

Skype has announced that in the first half of 2015 Lync will be rebranded as Skype for Business with a user interface consistent with Skype's and many value added features, such as managed conferencing, for a complete business grade service.

Summary

Microsoft's acquisition of Skype has provided tighter integration with its business products such as Office Online, incorporating Outlook.com, Office, and Lync. Essentially this integration brings Skype connectivity to individual applications without the need to use a Skype client.

Key Points

▓   Outlook.com and several of its complementary Office Online applications let you link to your Skype account so you can use Skype while checking your email or editing a document during a collaboration session.

▓   Skype Chat in Outlook.com requires no installation, but remembers that your chat history won't be visible and chat messages won't be buffered if your contact is offline.

▓   A browser plugin is necessary to make voice or video calls through Skype on Office Online modules.

▓   Outlook 2010 and 2013 now include integration with Skype such that Skype conversations can be launched and accessed from an Office contact header or the People module of Outlook.

Skype integration with Lync opens up a broader range of contacts with whom instant messaging and voice calling can occur.

Chapter **13**

The Way Ahead

This book has covered a lot of ground for the business or power professional or any individual who seeks out a low-cost worldwide communications service. Skype has extended the technology originally known as VoIP (Voice over Internet Protocol) to evolve into an IP-based communications tool that not only provides "free voice calling," but also makes it possible for people to build relationships, share experiences, host multi-party conversations (including voice and video) and, most importantly, build a business where geography is no longer a barrier to hiring employees, working with suppliers or, most critically, establishing a worldwide customer base.

After 11 years, Skype has matured in many ways. While it went from a startup through a couple of investment plays, most recently Skype has become a relatively independent business unit within Microsoft, supporting seven operating systems. Features beyond simply making voice and video connections will continue to be enhanced and introduced. In the quest to become more robust and reliable, a new backend infrastructure has evolved to the point where Skype can support text message buffering, file storage when sharing, and other features in more user-friendly ways.

But product maturity also means the quest for innovation becomes more difficult, especially when there is the need to ensure existing popular features need to be maintained. (Yes, several Skype features have come and gone, largely due to lack of interest, privacy and spam issues, and customer feedback). Every new user interface generates controversy; yet these changes make other features more effective.

Where Does Skype Go From Here?

We see Skype evolving with new features on Skype for mobile devices, including deeper integration into the overall mobile operating system to make Skype a feature equivalent alternative to carrier voice channel calling. Microsoft continues to enhance their Office and Xbox products with embedded Skype calling to support document collaboration activities. Lync—about to rebranded as Skype for Business with a new Skype-like user interface—is now being offered as a module in Office 365 online, supporting collaboration activities at a very low per seat cost. Skype has announced a beta Skype for Web—providing the ability to access Skype from within a web browser—useful when using PCs that do not have a Skype client installed.

Can Skype continue to build its user base with competition coming from Facebook (and their $22B WhatsApp investment), Google (and their expanding Hangouts features), and Apple's FaceTime? BlackBerry's BBM offers some interesting features such as complementing group chat with photo libraries, lists, and event coordination. BBM Meetings supports multiparty voice and video calls with up to 25 participants; meetings can be created and hosted on both mobile devices and PCs. (Full disclosure: the author used BBM on a recent month long trip to send daily "photo postcards" back to his family.)

Where do Internet-Based Communications Go From Here?

Possibly the highest profile activity involving IP-based communications is the attempt to develop a WebRTC standard—or more clearly the ability to initiate a conversation directly from within a web browser. But this is an activity that is ripe with challenges:

- ▨ WebRTC is a technology not a solution; it needs to be implemented within user applications embedded into web browsers. This involves embracing developer communities to incorporate it into websites, web applications, and, most challenging, mobile applications.

- ▨ What is the disruptive (business) pain that would necessitate WebRTC? Simply put it's about faster engagement—instantly join a conference call or answer a customer call without the pregnant pause that occurs while a connection is completed. And place that call directly from a web browser, ideally with no plugin installation required.

- Can the various players even come to an agreement on standards, especially with video codecs, which is the protocol required to make video calling work at all. It appears that both VP8 and H.264 are becoming required; however, VP9 and H.265 are under development.

  - The downside to H.26x is the requirement for royalties although Cisco has attempted to alleviate these when using Firefox.

  - H.264 is heavily embedded into many video hardware devices; this reduces the video processing load on PC and mobile device processors and was a driving force behind supporting both VP8 and H.264.

  - VP8 (and potentially VP9) are embedded into Google Chrome and Google Hangouts on a royalty-free basis.

- Can it become supported in all browsers? Currently the proposed WebRTC standard is supported in Firefox and Google Chrome but players such as Microsoft's Internet Explorer (along with Skype) are taking their own path while Apple is totally mum (as is usual) on the issue with respect to Safari implementation.

There is agreement on voice or audio codecs such that WebRTC-supported conversations incorporate the crystal-clear voice associated with Skype-to-Skype calls. In fact the primary standard includes the royalty-free SILK technology developed by Skype.

In summary, while WebRTC allows users to make calls and launch chat conversations directly from a web browser, it does require developer activity to embed call activation in each website or web application. Also developers need the appropriate tools to support WebRTC on mobile devices; these are only now slowly emerging. As a result, we will see slow ramp up of WebRTC usage (and Skype for Web activity) as developer exposure and support evolve.

From a business perspective, where the business wants to encourage immediate engagement directly from a website, WebRTC is suitable for conference calls, inbound customer sales, and support services (such as Amazon's Mayday service for Kindle owners) and possibly an involvement in the emerging Internet of Things. However, with its huge number of active users, Skype for Web also has the potential to be used for directly accessing Skype features from within a web browser.

Yet Skype clients and mobile applications provide a totally independent feature-rich communications-focused environment that can replace legacy voice and video calling.

Questions that arise include:

- Can live chat combined with WebRTC become the final blow to requiring a premise-based legacy business telephone system (PBX or private branch exchange) with an automated call answer directory for routing inbound calls to sales or service? This is partially driven by the fact that many call centers offer chat as a way to initiate engagement directly from a website; the WebRTC (and Skype for Web) opportunity is the ability to escalate to a voice or video call in context).

- Can a WebRTC voice call be combined with today's computerized automobile services to send car diagnostic information to a dealer immediately, from the "road," upon a component breakdown?

IP-Based Communications and the Traditional Telcos

While not apparent to the end user, most telecommunications service providers rely on IP-based communications technology to carry long distance calls to their destination. The user may experience it through offerings that provide unlimited calling within a country or mobile carrier's Home territory. For example Rogers wireless and landline services recently incorporated plans that include unlimited calling within Canada at little incremental cost, if any.

Where the consumer will notice a difference is where a provider implements HD Voice (incorporating Skype's SILK technology or an equivalent) to incorporate crystal-clear voice quality. For instance, Verizon and AT&T Mobility have introduced a service called VoLTE (Voice over LTE, a fourth generation network protocol) that has the potential to replace legacy mobile carrier voice channels. Currently it only works between customers on the same network; however, it is anticipated there will be cross network interoperability at some time in 2015.

Recall that placing Skype calls over wireless carriers uses the carriers' data networks and plans. VoLTE brings another change in that; it also operates over the carriers' data networks as opposed to the voice channel of earlier carrier protocols. This does place a significantly increased load onto the carrier's wireless network capacity.

EMERGENCY CALLING 911 AND ALL THAT

One area of contention for Skype has been emergency calling or, as it is called in North America, 911 services. At this point Skype states:

Skype Software is not a replacement for your ordinary mobile or fixed line telephone. In particular, apart from in very limited circumstances, the Software does not allow you to make emergency calls to emergency services. You must make alternative communication arrangements to ensure you can make emergency calls if necessary.

However, there is immense potential to make emergency calling more effective using IP-based technology. As a start, how about location identification when you make a call from a mobile device? Combining text chat, voice activation such as Siri, and other features could make emergency calling more effective. However, it's a case of telcos, software publishers, and public safety agencies working together to come up with an appropriate solution.

Guidelines for Evaluating the Evolution of IP-Based Communications

There are several new IP-based communication offerings emerging; however, over time very few have survived in the long term. When it comes to new offerings or upgrades to current offerings the questions I always ask include:

- Does it support crystal-clear voice and HD video calling?

- Is it available across all PCs, laptops, and multiple mobile devices?

- Does it support calling to landlines and mobile phones?

- Can calls be complemented with photo sharing, document sharing, and screen sharing?

- What is the level of support for multi-party calls?

  - Can multi-party calls be established, managed, and hosted only on PCs or also on mobile devices?

  - How many participants can be involved in a voice or video multi-party call?

- Does a multi-party call support participation by all on the call?

- Does a multi-party call support a "presentation" mode with a few active participants but a much larger listening audience?

- Is call activity logged or archived?

  - Can it be readily searched? How far back in time?

- Are chat sessions buffered such that offline parties can view previous messages sent while the party was offline?

- Are chat and logging activities mirrored onto other devices that support the same user account?

- And perhaps the most overriding question: Whom can I call? Who are my contacts and how much effort is required to build up a Contact directory?

  - Are there options to minimize spam calling?

Conclusion

My first experience with voice calling over the Internet was in 1996 when my employer of the day launched a voice calling application running over 43kbps dialup modems on PCs with 50MHz processors. Our developers were stressed out trying to just make it happen under these conditions. There was no directory service and the concept of Internet (chat) messaging had not been introduced. You would run the application and hope that somebody "out there" would actually answer using the same application.

In 2003 the Internet had matured to the point where the infrastructure was in place for a reliable, yet free, communications experience. Higher speed processors and broadband Internet had moved beyond their infancy. Two software pioneers had achieved the expertise to come up with an easy-to-install, robust, and innovative communications application. Internet messaging was already in its infancy while the concept of a Contacts directory was introduced. Skype was launched and became viral in adoption.

Twelve years later over 300 million use the current versions of Skype every month. And it has a rich feature set that incorporates HD video calling, crystal clear voice along with complementary features such as file transfer, screen sharing, voice and video messaging, along with others that make for a very productive communications ecosystem. And those calls can be handled on a wide range of intelligent hardware platforms—PC's, smartphones, tablets, and TVs—over both wired and wireless connections.

One of the reviews for the first edition of *Experience Skype to the Max* stated, "I didn't know what I didn't know." It is my hope that this edition not only brings you up to date on the full range of Skype features but also encourages you to find ways to turn Skype into a critical productivity tool for your business communications as well as a resource for supporting family and friend activity in today's very hyper-active, always connected world of work and play.

IP communications will continue to evolve; innovation is endemic to today's communications offerings. While the only application with communications as its core feature set across all multiple platforms, Skype will be competing with Facebook Messenger and Google Hangouts who want you to be able to launch a conversation directly from an email message or while viewing a Facebook post. The user interface continues to be a prime target for new ideas but the evolution of supporting hardware also presents new opportunities.

You can keep up with developments at Skype via the Skype Blogs (http://blogs.skype.com/) and at Voice On The Web (http://voiceontheweb.biz/) where I cover not only Skype but also other activity involving internet-based communications.

Now it's your turn—go ahead, place calls, share experiences and ideas, build business and family relationships, and seize benefit from a more connected world.

Glossary

While every attempt has been made to focus on the personal user experience while avoiding reference to technology terms and background, occasionally there are some terms that creep into any conversation or discussion about Skype that may need some clarification. Hopefully this Glossary provides some of that clarification.

3G – A term related to the speed of a wireless carrier's data service; means the carrier uses a third generation protocol that is significantly faster than 2G/EDGE protocols. HSPA and HSPA+ are faster enhanced versions of 3G. The most common protocol offered by wireless carriers after 2011; mobile phones offered in 2011 or later support at least 3G protocol.

4G/LTE – A term related to the speed of a wireless carrier's service; means a fourth generation protocol that is faster than 3G. Gradually introduced by carriers over the 2012–2014 time frame. Requires mobile phones that can support 4G/LTE; these include most phones launched during or after 2013. LTE is also the first protocol that is a common worldwide standard with a migration path from carriers who offered either GSM 3G or CDMA 3G.

Audio Terminology – Relates to the audio quality of a voice call resulting from limitations imposed by the connection between the parties on a call. As a guideline keep in mind that our ears can respond to (or hear) frequencies from 50 Hz to 22 KHz; the broader the audio frequency range supported in a voice call, the better the voice quality.

- *Narrowband:* Has been used by the landline carriers for decades resulting in the deterioration of voice quality when making a PSTN call relative to speaking face-to-face. Frequency range: 200 Hz to 3700 Hz (3.7 KHz); only captures the "fundamental" frequencies of your voice.

- *Wideband:* Used by Internet-based voice applications where there is a direct Internet connection between the parties on a call (i.e., the call does not go through a landline or mobile carrier at any point). Provides much better voice quality due to picking up the "harmonics" of your voice; frequency range ~100 Hz to 7.5-8 KHz. Results in fewer "can you repeat that" and clearer handling of accents.

- *Superwideband:* Was initially introduced with the launch of Skype's SILK voice technology. Provides the crystal-clear audio quality heard on any Skype-to-Skype call, including video calls. Frequency range: ~50 Hz to 12 KHz.

Carrier – A more technical term for a traditional phone company that connects and carries landline and/or wireless (mobile) voice conversations. Rogers, Bell Canada, Telus, AT&T, Verizon, British Telecom (BT), and Deutsche Telecomm are examples of carriers.

HD Video – Equivalent of one of two HDTV video resolutions: 720p (1280 × 720) or 1080p (1920 × 1080). HD Video resolutions require faster upload speeds than High Quality Video.

High Quality Video – Video delivered at 640 × 480 resolution and 24 frames-per-second.

Internet Bandwidth – Refers to the speeds at which data is delivered over an Internet connection, with separate download and upload speeds. Usually the download speed is significantly higher than upload speed but they may become close to equal on, say, fiber-based connections. For Skype the minimum and recommended speeds are:

Call Type	Minimum download/upload speeds	Recommended download/upload speeds
Voice	30kbps/30kbps	100kbps/100kbps
Video	128 kbps/128kbps	300kbps/300kbps
High Quality Video	400 kbps/400kbps	500kbps/500kbps
HD Video	1.2Mbps/1.2Mbps	1.5Mbps/1.5Mbps
Group Video (3 participants)	512kbps/128kbps	2Mbps/512Mbps
Group Video (5 participants)	2Mbps/128kbps	4Mbps/512kbps
Group Video (7+ Participants)	4Mbps/128kbps	8Mbps/512kbps

Over-the-Top (OTT) Communications – Text, voice, and video communications services that are carried directly between PCs and smartphones using the inherent Internet infrastructure for transporting data packets, bypassing the traditional landline and wireless carriers as service providers.

PC or Personal Computer – Any desktop or laptop computer that uses the Windows, Mac OS X or, in some cases, Linux operating system.

Peer-to-Peer – An Internet software technology where two or more parties are connected directly (without any "server" support) to carry out a transaction or real time conversation. This is the core technology that allows Skype-to-Skype calls and conversations to be "free"; it has also been used for file sharing.

POTS – Plain old telephone service (see PSTN).

Presence – An indication of your current status for receiving Skype calls: Online, Away, Do Not Disturb, Offline, etc. that is seen by your Skype Contacts in the Skype Contact directory within their Skype client. On Android, BlackBerry 10 and Windows Phone devices presence only has two options: Available, Invisible.

PSTN – Public switched telephone network. The legacy landline and wireless voice communications services where calls are essentially made by dialing a number comprising a country code, area code, and local number.

Roaming charges – Wireless carrier fees for use of a smartphone over carrier networks outside the user's "home" network. Usually quite expensive relative to the charges for the same services on a user's home carrier network.

Skype – A real-time communications software application that takes advantage of the Internet's underlying technology to support free or low cost text, voice, and video conversations worldwide.

Skype Account – Manages your Skype subscriptions and "Pay-As-You-Go" payments (call phones, SMS messaging) and calling features such as voice mail, call forwarding, callerID, Skype To Go numbers, and Skype Online number(s).

Skype Client – The Skype software application installed on a PC, smartphone, tablet, or other device.

Skype Credit – Skype's "currency" used for prepaying for SkypeOut calls, SMS messages, and other offerings on a "Pay-As-You-Go" basis. Fund your Skype Account with Skype credit in amounts of $10.00 or $30.00 or similar amounts in other currencies. Credits are then used as you make calls that require a "per call" payment. (Check out Skype Calling Plans for fixed cost subscriptions.)

Skype Online Number – A phone number that can be called from a landline or mobile phone (PSTN) to reach a Skype user on a Skype client.

SkypeOut – The Skype offering that allows you to make calls from a Skype client on a PC, mobile smartphone, tablet or other device to landlines and wireless phones (or to the PSTN). Charges and calling plan subscriptions apply. Now called "Calls to Landlines and Mobile Phone".

Skype Profile – Your personal registration information directly associated with your Skype activity: SkypeID, Picture (Avatar), First Name, Last Name, and many optional items, including Location (City, Country), Home/Work/Mobile phone numbers, website address, time zone, birthday, etc.

Smartphone – Any mobile phone that can supports applications that require the Internet for delivering and receiving information in the form of data delivered by a wireless carrier. Often referred to as a mobile PC, due to the proliferation of applications now available for smartphones.

VoLTE – with the availability of very fast 4G/LTE carrier services for data, Voice over LTE will use the data channel to complement or even replace the legacy voice channel. With VoLTE support carriers can take advantage of superwideband audio for significantly improved voice quality.

VoIP – Voice Over Internet Protocol. This is the generic term for the technology behind the ability to place voice (and video) calls over the Internet. It involves digitizing a voice (or video image) at the sending end for transmitting the audio (or video) content over the Internet and decoding the digital information back to an audio voice or video image at the receiving end, all in real time.

WebRTC – An evolving technology to allow chat, voice and video conversations to be launched directly from a website or web application, In effect it would support these conversations without the need to use a separate client or application.

Wi-Fi – An unregulated wireless protocol that allows connections to the Internet over a short range (less than 50 meters) from a Wi-Fi access point. Used for connecting Wi-Fi–enabled PCs and devices to the Internet via local area networks (at home or a business operation) or Wi-Fi hotspots at airports, restaurants, coffee shops, hotels, and other road warrior locations. Often referred to as the "stealth" carrier as Wi-Fi is usually associated with free or low-cost wireless Internet connections that can be substituted for expensive wireless carrier roaming connections when traveling outside the home country.

Index

Get the eBook for only $10!

> Now you can take the weightless companion with you anywhere, anytime. Your purchase of this book entitles you to 3 electronic versions for only $10.

This Apress title will prove so indispensible that you'll want to carry it with you everywhere, which is why we are offering the eBook in 3 formats for only $10 if you have already purchased the print book.

Convenient and fully searchable, the PDF version enables you to easily find and copy code—or perform examples by quickly toggling between instructions and applications. The MOBI format is ideal for your Kindle, while the ePUB can be utilized on a variety of mobile devices.

Go to www.apress.com/promo/tendollars to purchase your companion eBook.

49449159R00147

Made in the USA
Lexington, KY
06 February 2016